TECHNOLOGY MANAGEMENT

TECHNOLOGY MANAGEMENT

APPLICATIONS TO CORPORATE MARKETS AND MILITARY MISSIONS

GEORGE K. CHACKO

PRAEGER

New York
Westport, Connecticut
London

*Soc
HD
45
C44
1988*

Library of Congress Cataloging-in-Publication Data

Chacko, George Kuttickal, 1930-
   Technology management: applications to corporate markets and
military missions/George K. Chacko.
      p.   cm.
   Bibliography: p.
   Includes index.
   ISBN 0-275-92941-8 (alk. paper)
   1. Technological innovations—Management.   2. High technology
industries—Management.   3. Technological innovations—Marketing.
4. High technology—Marketing.   5. High technology industries—
Military aspects.   6. Technology transfer.   I. Title.
HD45.C44 1988
620'.0068—dc 19   88–12029

Library of Congress Catalog Card Number: 88–12029
ISBN: 0-275-92941–8

First published in 1988

Praeger Publishers, One Madison Avenue, New York, NY 10010
A division of Greenwood Press, Inc.

Printed in the United States of America

The paper used in this book complies with the
Permanent Paper Standard issued by the National
Information Standards Organization (Z39.48–1984).

10   9   8   7   6   5   4   3   2   1

Dedicated affectionately to

ASHIA

Our daughter, the artist

Who may well discern in

This scientific work on the

Art of managing high technology

A portrait of the possible

Contents

Tables and Figures

TABLES

FIGURES

Preface

The survival of mankind hanging on the slim thread of high technology (hi-tech) is highlighted in President Reagan's speech proposing the Strategic Defense Initiative (SDI), dubbed "Star Wars":

What if free people could live secure in the knowledge that their security did not rest upon the threat of instant U.S. retaliation to deter a Soviet attack, that we could intercept and destroy strategic ballistic missiles before they reached our own soil or that of our allies?[1]

Whether or not ballistic missiles can be intercepted and destroyed in the preboost, boost, postboost, or terminal phase is not currently known. However, the very journey toward that hi-tech frontier has had a dramatic effect upon what Herman Khan first called "thinking about the unthinkable."[2]

Survival of quite a different kind, namely, survival in the marketplace, is also very much dictated by hi-tech. The sudden surfacing in 1985 of the United States as a net debtor to the world for the first time in three generations to the tune of $150 billion, and the feasible though frightening scenario of a $1-trillion trade deficit by 1989, demand that an effective way be found to cut the spiral of deficits.

The trade deficit is a symptom of the underlying trade drain, the international imbalance among the elements of the triad of instruction, invention, and innovation. Unbridled competition aggravates this imbalance, but competition in some elements and cooperation in other elements ameliorates it.

Formally called "concomitant coalition" (CONCOL), this approach of competitive cooperation recognizes that the participants in an activity ("players in the game") can work with and against the same party in the same activity. For instance, to acquire as much of the global market as possible, the corporation (country) can lose some part of the market in order to gain some other part. Or, it may choose to lose some part of today's market in order to gain some other part of tomorrow's market.

Interestingly enough, an example of CONCOL applicable to the market is provided by a real-life instance of the military mission, the "game" of nuclear survival. The United States is with France but against the Soviet Union because the United States and France are members of the North Atlantic Treaty Organization (NATO), which the Soviet Union cannot join. Survival of nuclear war by averting it is NATO's objective, an objective shared by the signatories of the 1963 partial Test Ban Treaty. Yet in the very same "game" of nuclear survival, the same players reverse their associations: the United States is against France but with the Soviet Union on the Test Ban Treaty, because the United States and the Soviet Union are signatories, while France is not.

It is the thesis of thesis book that CONCOL offers a viable concept of technology management to improve survival, both of markets and mankind.

The first part of this book develops the factual basis of the competition for scientists and engineers for missions and markets, both intra- and internationally.

Chapter 1 underscores the primary assignment of technology management: survival of the country and of the corporation. If country and corporate survival hinges on hi-tech, particularly the unborn kind, how should resources be committed to assure survival? We look at four historic decisions relating to missions (radar in Great Britain, the Manhattan Project in the United States, the Apollo Project, and Star Wars) and two relating to markets (semiconductors/Texas Instruments, 360/IBM).

Chapter 2 discusses the implications of the fact that a dollar committed to Research and Development for missions is a dollar denied to R&D for markets, and vice versa. Of the three categories of R&D, development is closest to the industry's heart, because it gets the products to the market. To sustain development, basic research is critical. An empirical measure is developed to tell us how good our R&D mix is: the Innovation/Invention (O/V) ratio. To sustain R&D, the infrastructure is vital. Five new empirical indices of R&D are developed: (1) monetary measure of basic research; (2) numerical measure of potential inventors; (3) number and cost of potential inventors; (4) degree and discipline of potential inventors; and (5) share of military R&D.

Chapter 3 develops a concept which provides the framework to allocate funds between opposing interests, such as country and corporate R&D, mission and market R&D, and present and potential products. To make the CONCOL concept operational, we develop five technology outcome measures and four territory outcome measures.

Chapter 4 presents the portents of the Japanese sweep of the world market for hi-tech products, which can, in extreme cases, lead to the United States denying to Japan the (market) territory for its technology. Japan's "ceramic fever" has implications not merely for the $10-billion industry, but also for sensitive military missions because of ceramics application to integrated circuits. Integrated circuits are vital to the survival of the United States. Using the U.S.-Soviet technology scorecard in 20 basic technology areas, a basis is developed for allocation of resources to three armed services.

The second part of this book examines the elements of the CONCOL foundation of the Decision to Dare, committing significant segments of country/corporate resources.

Chapter 5 develops the elements of the Decision to enhance the probability of corporate/country survival. Whether it relates to corporations or countries, commitment of resources for results must recognize the technology transformation track (3T), time frame, and resources risk ratio (3R), which classify decisions into D-positive, D-negative, and D-zero.

Chapter 6 incorporates these three elements to classify the decisions, and analyzes three successful historic Decisions to Dare (TI—semiconductors; Haloid—Xerox; Roosevelt—Manhattan Project) using an analytical framework made up of technological gleam, market design, and financial risk.

Chapter 7 examines the failure of a mission (Hitler's decision not to develop the atomic bomb) and the failure of a market (RCA's decision to cling to vacuum tube Nuvistors), and discusses the validity of the analytical framework in reinforcing the anecdotal.

The third part of this book develops the requirements of technology and territory forecasts, and noting the need for highly accurate adaptive forecasts, discusses several applications of a new numerical forecasting method, MESGRO (Modified Exponential Smoothing-GROwth).

Chapter 8 examines the question, Who should specify the improved/invented product characteristics—the user or the inventor? Forecasting methods appropriate to forecast linear extensions of performance characteristics and quantum jumps are discussed.

Chapter 9 presents a new, computer-based, numerical forecasting method which uses few data points to forecast accurately, and adapts quickly to wide fluctuations. Several of the 45 applications of MESGRO are discussed.

The final part of this book presents the CONCOL bargaining process, which moves parties from opposing corners to middle ground where they can negotiate.

Chapter 10 develops three elements of the CONCOL process from the Cuban missile crisis, and applies it to the illegal sale of U.S. hi-tech by Japan to the Soviet Union.

Chapter 11 develops the corporate strategy to harmonize the interests of improvement of products and invention of new products from the point of view of their inherent conflicts. How the heavy investment in R&D by large corporations, such as multinationals, could use technology transfer to newly industrializing countries (NICs) as a mutually beneficial CONCOL is discussed.

This work is designed for those who manage technology for missions and for those who manage technology for markets. The former would work in and for the military, space, and communications agencies. The latter would work in and for corporations which sell products and services.

The self-contained treatment of this work, and its 15 real-life applications, it is hoped, will commend it to students from several disciplines in schools of business, systems, and technology:

Business management	Corporate long-range planning
Technology management	Project management
R&D management	Technology transfer
Technological forecasting	Trade and technology

This work is suitable for a one- or two-semester graduate or advanced undergraduate course; and it offers an integrated point of departure for serious discussion of one of the most significant issues of our times.

Part I

Invention versus Innovation—The Continuing Conflict

1

The Twin Imperatives of Technology Management

OVERVIEW: Nothing less than the very survival of the country and the corporation is the charge of technology management. To fulfill this mandate, the technology manager manages technology, or rather, high technology (hi-tech).

Hi-tech underlines human survival in the nuclear age. In 1988 the prospects of human survival are hitched to the star of a hi-tech that is years away from being born—Star Wars. Corporate survival, just as much as country survival, depends on hi-tech. Japan's cornering of 90 percent of the world's market of 256 kilobit D-RAMS, long before they are manufactured commercially, sends U.S. chip manufacturers scrambling for survival.

If country and corporate survival hinges on hi-tech, particularly the unborn kind, how should resources be committed to assure survival? Obviously, there is no foolproof method of research and development (R&D) decision making. Can experience teach us? We will look at four dramatic decisions relating to missions and two relating to markets. In all instances, the decision was to invent hi-tech. The risk was very great: survival of the nation (radar for Great Britain; the atomic bomb for the United States; SDI for the United States); survival of national prestige (the moon landing for the United States); or survival of the corporation (semiconductors for Texas Instruments; third-generation computers for IBM).

SURVIVAL ON TWO FRONTS

The technology manager (TM) is charged with survival. He or she is judged by one criterion: *survival of the country or the corporation.*

Country Survival: Mission

Our focus is technology—in fact, hi-tech. Its use to further country survival is hard to identify and assess because we know survival best when it is gone—too late. Therefore, we have to develop surrogate measures to detect tendencies toward nonsurvival.

As Hamlet says, "Aye, there's the rub." We can disagree honestly about survival and its surrogates. Winston Churchill was a voice in the wilderness during the pre-World War II years, when he was powerless and alone; his early warnings of Britain's possible nonsurvival were ignored and ridiculed by those in high places. Only when "the gathering storm" broke upon a totally unprepared Britain did the country turn to her unheeded prophet.

In our day, the stakes are much steeper. While Churchill could make do with a holding action for two years, until he could persuade the United States to enter the war and jointly fight Hitler for another four years, today there will be no six years of strategic nuclear war. Survival ticks off in seconds and minutes. If our satellites sense the launch of Soviet strategic missiles, the maximum warning time is about 15 minutes. Despite intense efforts during the intervening decades, that tiny window has remained virtually unchanged since the 1950s.

While averting strategic nuclear war is a political process, we are here concerned with hi-tech underpinnings that can make or break it. For instance, Eisenhower's proposal for "open skies" could not be implemented until technology provided the means to detect underground nuclear tests from space. The indispensable underpinnings of technology were again recognized in 1985 at the Reagan–Gorbachev Geneva summit, where Gorbachev proposed access to laboratories—which we may call "open laboratories."

Survival is not static; its scope is altered by hi-tech which makes possible feats unimagined until recently. In the 1960s, a Soviet Intercontinental Ballistic Missile (ICBM) could expect to hit a target within a thousand miles; in the 1980s, it can strike within a thousand feet. This 5000-fold improvement in accuracy could be pursued by the United States and the Soviet Union because such a dramatic breakthrough was inconceivable at the time of Strategic Arms Limitation Talks (SALT).

How can we differentiate between hi-tech designed to further survival of the country from that furthering survival of the corporation? An all-or-nothing result applies to country survival, while a whole range of values of return-on-investment (ROI) are acceptable as outcomes to corporate survival. Country survival is the concern of *Missions*; corporate survival is the concern of *Markets*.

Corporate Survival: Market

Robots, more than cars, are on GM Chairman Smith's mind:

"I've got a question in my mind" says [Roger E.] Smith. "Do we need anything more in that area? . . . There's enough horses in that field out there for nine races, and I don't just want to win one race. So maybe we have to go out there and get a couple of more horses. I don't think I know right now that I want to say, 'Okay, I made my bet on GM-Fanuc. It could run in the sixth at the Belmont, and that's all I've ever got to do to be the biggest horseman in the country.' "[1]

The *Washington Post* interview of Smith and others at General Motors clearly indicates that the "field" is by no means limited to the manufacture and sale of factory robots and robotics. If anything, the field is limited only by imagination, ingenuity, and investment.

If expanding into markets offered by new technologies such as robotics is a relatively new venture for GM, betting on future technology has been the style of TRW, described by the *Financial Times* as "a rather unusual blend of the familiar and the fabulous—from satellites and semiconductors to steering wheels and submergible pumps."[2] TRW, which achieved its 1961 goal to reach the $1-billion mark before the decade was out with 1967 net sales of $1,040,942, looks to an ever-increasing share of future revenues to come from products which are not yet on the drawing board. Ruben F. Mettler, chief executive officer (CEO), speaks of TRW growth through new markets:

TRW is a multidimensional company that throughout its history has shown the ability to anticipate promising new fields and to pioneer in their development—from automotive, industrial, aviation, aerospace, systems engineering, electronics, and energy. *The company grew with those markets, and indeed, helped create them.* [emphasis added][3]

He illustrates the creation of new markets as follows:

International sales have increased from zero in the early 1960s to about 33 percent of the total revenues today. And energy programs, which were non-existent in the early 1960s, now represent more than 10 percent of sales....In the electronics and space systems segment, TRW is one of a select few firms on the leading edge of several important new technologies. To cite just a few, TRW is involved in microelectronics and fiber optics for advanced communications devices; scientific spacecraft that increase man's understanding of the heavens; communications satellites that send messages all over the world; and powerful computer chips that contain more than 200,000 parts on a surface only one-quarter inch square.[4]

It is important to note that the new technologies are clearly to promote new products, ranging from computer chips to spacecraft. The company grows with these markets and helps create them. These markets are not merely domestic; they are global. One out of three revenue dollars comes from international sales.

Since the United States is the best market for most products and services, it is no small wonder that even as U.S. firms reach out to other markets, other countries reach out to the U.S. market. An example of a phenomenal success in this regard is Japan. Commenting on Japan's national commitment to the fifth-generation computer system, one of the fathers of artificial intelligence (AI),

Edward Feigenbaum of Stanford University, points out the effective challenges of Japan to U.S. survival in the markets for automobiles, electronics (including video tape recorders), and semiconductors:

We now regret our complacency in other technologies. Who in the 1960s took seriously Japanese initiatives in small cars? Who in 1970 took seriously the Japanese national goal to become number one in consumer electronics in ten years? (Have you seen an American VTR that isn't Japanese on the inside?) In 1972, when the Japanese had yet to produce their first commercial microelectronics chip but announced plans in this vital "made in America" technology, who would have thought in ten years they would have half of the world market in memory chips?[5]

When it comes to semiconductors, the issue is not just the loss of a few million dollars of sales. As the chips are not peripheral to products, but indeed foundational, whoever dominates the microchip market has gone a long way toward dominating the products and processes built on chips—ranging from computers to satellites, and calculators to consumer electronics. The Japanese success in the microchip market definitely challenges the United State's very survival, in not only the chips market, but more importantly, in the market for all products and processes for which the chips are an input. The approach to R&D in the United States and Japan in the semiconductor industry is so strikingly different that prospects of an early or effective reversal of the Japanese conquest are at best doubtful:

Analysts say good quality and low prices have helped Japanese win two-thirds of the world market for standard dynamic random access memory (D-RAM) chips of 64 kilobits.

Japanese chips have also won 90 percent of the market for the newest generation of 256-kilobit D-RAMs. Many analysts say Japan is poised to capture the market for one-megabit D-RAMs, the next generation of increased capacity memory chips.

Americans may still have an edge in making semi-custom and custom design chips which require sophisticated computer software capability, the analysts say. But rising Japanese investment in research and development may put even this field at risk.

"If they can dominate the memory chip market, they can use the *cash generated from it for research and development* and new facilities," Christian Wignall, managing director of G.T. Management (Japan) Ltd. told Reuters.

Differences in the structure of U.S. and Japanese semiconductor makers has been a key factor in Japan's growing market share. "*U.S. firms are pure chip makers, while Japanese firms all have alternative business* so they can take the cash flow from other sectors to keep their semiconductor business going," Wignall said. [emphasis added] [6]

Return on investment is a standard measure of success in the marketplace. However, before there can be any return, there has to be a market. What we have seen is that U.S. survival is threatened in both the present and potential markets—the present market for memory chips and the potential market for products built on chips. We may refer to the technology underpinnings of corporate survival in terms of the *market*, even as we epitomize country survival dependent on technology as *mission*.

BETTING COUNTRY/CORPORATE SURVIVAL ON TECHNOLOGICAL BREAKTHROUGHS

The twin imperatives of technology management are country survival and corporate survival.

During the 43 years from May 10, 1940 through March 23, 1983, four dramatic decisions to risk the very survival of the country on yet-to-be-proven technological breakthroughs have been made on both sides of the Atlantic. We will briefly examine these decisions for their lessons for technology management. They are instances of the application of technology management. We will identify them as *mission applications* since the focus is missions, rather than markets. We will also sketch two dramatic decisions to risk the very survival of the corporation on yet-to-be-proven technological breakthroughs. We will identify these as *market applications* since the focus is markets.

MISSION APPLICATION 1: REWRITING AIR DEFENCE AROUND UNBORN RADAR

The Decision

Winston Churchill said: "The plans for the air defence of Great Britain had, as early as the autumn of 1937, been rewritten round the assumption that the promises made by our scientists for the still unproven radar would be kept." [7]

The Mission

During 1934–1935 Great Britain lost air parity to Germany. On June 7, 1935, Churchill pressed upon the House of Commons the critical need to invent the technology to be warned of approaching enemy aircraft:

It is concerned with the methods which can be *invented or adopted or discovered* to enable the earth to control the air, to enable defence from ground to exercise control—indeed domination—upon airplanes high above its surface . . . .My experience is that in these matters, when the *need is fully explained* by military and political authorities, Science is always able to provide something. [emphasis added] [8]

It was quite revolutionary to postulate that air space could be controlled, and even dominated from the ground. Only after a new prime minister took office did Churchill get a chance to work on the new Committee of Imperial Defence on Air Defence Research, which he was to do for the next four years during the life of the committee.

The Resources

An admitted layperson, Churchill had to rely on his confidant, Professor Frederick Lindemann. "Lindemann could decipher the signals from the experts on the far horizons and explain to me in lucid, homely terms what the issues were." [9] With Lindemann's technical advice, Churchill moved resolutely to provide all the necessary funds and resources to invent the new technology:

When in 1940, the chief responsibility fell upon me and our *national survival depended upon victory in the air*, I had the advantage of a layman's insight into the problems of air warfare resulting from four long years of study and thought based upon the fullest official and technical information. [emphasis added] [10]

What I had to grasp were the practical results, and just as Lindemann gave me his views for all it was worth in the field, so I made sure by *turning on my power-relay* that some at least of these terrible and incomprehensible truths emerged in executive decisions. [emphasis added] [11]

The Decision

Churchill was convinced that when the need is explained, science will respond with the answer. His scientific advisor interpreted for him the signals from the far horizon of scientific possibilities. As soon as he got the power, Churchill ensured that adequate resources were devoted to inventing the new technology.

MISSION APPLICATION 2: "TO SEE THAT THE NAZIS DON'T BLOW US UP"

Five months before Winston Churchill became prime minister of Great Britain, President Franklin D. Roosevelt made a momentous decision that was to change forever the landscape of hi-tech and of human history itself.

The Decision

Physicist Leo Szilard, a noted refugee from Hungary, became convinced in 1939 that a nuclear chain reaction could be sustained. The spectre of a German atomic bomb made Szilard shudder about survival. He composed a letter (both long and short versions) which Albert Einstein signed and (the longer version of) which Dr. Alexander Sachs took to Roosevelt on October 11, 1939. As their meeting drew to a close, Roosevelt remarked, "Alex, what you are after is to see that the Nazis don't blow us up."[12]

Roosevelt told his secretary, General Edwin M. Watson, "This requires action." Sachs left the room with Watson and by evening a small group of men was set up with the director of the U.S. Bureau of Standards, Dr. Lyman J. Briggs, as chairman.

The Mission

The mission of the Briggs Committee was to invent the technology of the atomic bomb. Einstein's letter of August 9 to Roosevelt suggested that nuclear fission was a technical possibility:

In the course of the *last four months* it has been made probable—through the work of Joliot in France as well as Fermi and Szilard in America—that it may become possible to set up nuclear chain reactions in a large mass of uranium, by which a vast amount of power and large quantities of new radium-like elements would be generated. Now it appears *almost certain* that this could be achieved in the *immediate* future. [emphasis added][13]

If it was revolutionary to postulate in 1937 that the air could be controlled from the ground, and even dominated, it was far more preposterous to suggest in 1939 that vast amounts of power could be generated from nuclear fission in the immediate future, when four years later, a physicist of Niels Bohr's eminence concluded: "I have, to the best of my judgment, convinced myself that in spite of all future prospects any *immediate use* of the latest marvelous discoveries of atomic physics *is impracticable.*" [emphasis added][14]

The Resources

The initial allocation to the Briggs Committee was only $200,000 to support research on methods of production of sufficient quantities of fissionable material for an atomic bomb. On December 6, 1941, the Office of Scientific Research and Development (OSRD) directed by Dr. Vannever Bush, replaced the Briggs Committee. Roosevelt wanted OSRD's recommendation on the choice from among the five methods of large-scale production of uranium. The chairman of the Atomic Committee of OSRD, Dr. James B. Conant, President of Harvard University, suggested that all five methods be pursued at a cost of $500 million which was 20 times the annual budget of Harvard.

The cost of the Manhattan Project has been placed at $2 billion—$2,191,000,000 to be exact; which is quite significant considering the $1,182,000,000 appropriations for the army and navy together, requested by Roosevelt on May 16, 1940.[15]

The Decision

"To see that the Nazis don't blow us up" epitomizes the need to invent nuclear technology. Einstein's stature made his incredible affirmation the firm foundation of Roosevelt's commitment to ensure the country's and the free world's survival.

MISSION APPLICATION 3: "BEFORE THIS DECADE IS OUT . . . LAND A MAN ON THE MOON AND RETURN HIM SAFELY TO THE EARTH"

From the gigantic gambles on technological breakthroughs for the physical survival of the country, we turn to the survival of national prestige (prestige survival).

The Decision

The successful "first" of cosmonaut Yuri Gagarin's flight in space on April 12, 1961, and the Bay of Pigs fiasco on April 17, 1961, imposed on the young, new president the need to extricate himself and the nation from the shattering assaults upon the self-image of the United States as the leader of the free world and the leader in science and technology.

John F. Kennedy addressed Congress on May 25, urging the nation to lay its prestige on the line in full glare of world publicity, and gamble that it would achieve the required technological breakthrough to go where no man had gone before: "I believe this nation should commit itself to achieving the goal, before this decade is out, of landing a man on the moon and returning him safely to the earth." [16]

The Mission

Two days after the Gagarin flight, President Kennedy met with Theodore Sorensen, Jerome Wiesner, David Bell, James Webb, and Hugh Dryden. Present at the meeting was Hugh Sidey of *Life* magazine. Sidey's report, which was checked by Kennedy for accuracy, shows that he was most concerned about the technological feasibility of catching up with or overtaking the Russians. "Now, let's look at this," said Kennedy impatiently. "Is there any place we can catch them? What can we do? Can we go around the moon before them? *Can we put a man on the moon before them?* (emphasis added). [17]

Political desirability, by itself, would not establish technological feasibility. Kennedy's memorandum of April 20, 1961 specifically asked for the technological feasibility of a space mission which would promise "dramatic results in which we could win." Thanks to the work of the National Aeronautics and Space Administration (NASA), especially under Dr. George Low's leadership dating back to 1959, Dr. Werner von Braun could tell Vice President Johnson a month before President Kennedy's address, on April 29, that there was a sporting chance of sending a three-man crew around the moon ahead of the Soviets, and an excellent chance of landing a man on the moon ahead of them.

The Resources

Unlike the Manhattan Project, the space program had at least a ten-year life envisaged at the outset. Therefore, the commitment of resources would be virtually open-ended. NASA's request for fiscal year 1964 (FY64) was for $5.7 billion, nearly six times the final Republican space budget. The cost of the lunar landing mission was about ten times that of the Manhattan Project ($25 billion).

The Decision

Unlike the Manhattan Project, Project Apollo was carried out in the full glare of world publicity. Every launch was well advertised and carried out in full view of the whole world. Kennedy inspired the nation to dare to reach outside existing technological horizons, and provided the resources to carry out the quest, the successful accomplishment of which reestablished national prestige.

MISSION APPLICATION 4: "INTERCEPT AND DESTROY STRATEGIC BALLISTIC MISSILES BEFORE THEY REACH OUR OWN SOIL OR THAT OF OUR ALLIES"

The decision to invent space technology of a different kind, namely non-nuclear defense that could render strategic nuclear missiles obsolete, underlies President Reagan's Strategic Defense Initiative (SDI), dubbed "Star Wars."

The Decision

Saying that "new technologies are now at hand which may make possible a truly effective non-nuclear defense," Reagan took the first step toward moving away from a future that depends on massive nuclear retaliation, and moving toward reliance on defensive systems:

On March 23, 1983, I announced my decision to take an important first step toward this goal by directing the establishment of a comprehensive and intensive research program, the Strategic Defense Initiative, aimed at eventually eliminating the threat posed by nuclear armed ballistic missiles.[18]

The Mission

When the Anti-Ballistic Missile (ABM) Treaty was signed in 1972, defense was confined to attacking nuclear warheads during the terminal phase as they swoop down on targets. It is now conceivable that emerging technologies may make it possible to have a layered defense. Figure 1.1 presents the boost, post-boost, and terminal phases. *Spectrum*, the journal of the Institute of Electric and Electronic Engineers, describes the computer simulation:

Fig. 1.1
SDI: Layered Defense

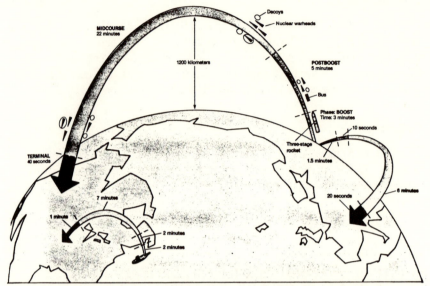

During its 31-minute intercontinental flight from the Soviet Union to the United States, a nuclear missile would go through four distinct phases. The rocket lifts off in the boost phase, burning for 3 minutes for an MX-like missile. At about 200 kilometers, the third-stage booster burns out. The missile is well beyond the earth's atmosphere and can begin to deploy its warheads and decoys from a spacecraft-like "bus" in frictionless space. During this 5-minute postboost phase, the bus uses thrusters to make small adjustments to its trajectory. After each precise adjustment it releases a warhead and perhaps tens of decoys. While in the long mid-course portion of the flight, the warheads and decoys travel on ballistic trajectories, reaching as high as 1200 kilometers. As the warheads reenter the atmosphere in the brief terminal phase, they heat up and the lighter decoys slow down and burn up. The length of each phase varies. Intermediate-range ballistic missiles (arc at right) and submarine-launched missiles (arc at left) travel through the same four stages, but their terminal phases are of different durations. Fast-burn boosters could reduce the time for boost-phase interception to less than 1 minute. Similarly, by releasing warheads and decoys in "clusters," the time for postboost deployment could be lowered to 10 seconds. But the changes have penalties for the offense.

Source: John A. Adam and Paul Wallich, "Mind-boggling Complexity,"
IEEE *Spectrum*, Sep '85, 37 © 1985 IEEE

In a simulation exercise like the one done by researcher Christopher T. Cunningham at Lawrence Livermore National Laboratory, it seems almost easy. A salvo of 1400 intercontinental ballistic missiles is fired on the screen, confronting a strategic defense system. Ninety percent of the missiles are picked off by laser battle stations in the *boost phase*, before they deploy their warheads and penetration aids. The *second* defensive *tier* destroys 90 percent of the remaining 10 percent of the missiles; the *third* and final *tier* is 90 percent effective against the rest of those that leak through. Overall effectiveness of the system: 99.9 percent. [emphasis added][19]

If SDI establishes the feasibility of such a system, a future president and Congress will have the technical knowledge to decide whether to develop such a system. A third decision is whether to deploy such a system.

"It Can't Be Done!"

Unlike the other three mission applications, the outcome of this decision is not yet known. What is known is that every new idea has been met with a chorus of reasons why it cannot be done.

Churchill talks about the unfortunate affirmation by the British prime minister foreswearing any technology that could dominate the aircraft:

Early in 1935, an Air Ministry Committee composed of scientists was set up and instructed to *explore the future*. We remembered that it was upon the advice of the Air Ministry that Mr. Baldwin had made the speech which produced so great an impression in 1933 when he said that *there was really no defence*. "The bomber will always get through." We had, therefore, *no confidence in any Air Ministry departmental committee*, and thought the subject should be transferred from the Air Ministry to the Committee of Imperial Defence, where the heads of the Government, the most powerful politicians in the country, would be able to supervise and superintend its actions and also to make sure that the *necessary funds* were not denied. [emphasis added][20]

Churchill underscores two elements critical to the success of the decision to invent technological breakthrough: right organization and adequate resources.

SDI Organization

SDI was established in January 1984 to carry out research in five areas: (1) surveillance, acquisition, tracking, and kill assessment (SATKA); (2) directed energy weapons (DEW) technologies; (3) kinetic energy weapons (KEW) technologies; (4) systems concepts/battle management (SC/BM); and (5) survivability, lethality, and key technologies (SLKT).[21]

It bears repetition that the charter of SDI is research. It is critical that the organization be led by a believer in the not-yet-proven technology and that the program should have a high priority. Both these essentials are fulfilled as the director of SDI, Lt. Gen. James A. Abrahamson, told Congress on October 30, 1985:

I cannot overstate *my commitment* to this crucial program and my conviction that it is of the utmost importance to our nation. Indeed, Secretary Weinberger has assigned the SDI the *highest priority* within the Department of Defense. [emphasis added][22]

The Resources

In its first year (FY85), SDI was allocated $1400 million. In spite of usual startup difficulties, SDI was able to maintain an obligation rate of 95 percent. Figure 1.2 shows the comparative funding levels in the first three years of SDI and the two High National priority programs—the Manhattan Project and the Apollo Program.

The Decision

Reagan made a dramatic break from the idea that balance of terror would stay the hand of nuclear destruction. That departure is predicated on an unproven technological breakthrough. But he has put his prestige behind the decision to invent the technological breakthrough and has backed it with adequate resources.

MARKET APPLICATION 1: "DEFINITE COMMITMENT TO DEVELOP, MANUFACTURE, AND MARKET SEMICONDUCTOR DEVICES"

From four *mission* applications, we turn to two *market* applications of gambling corporate survival on unproven technological breakthroughs.

The Decision

Texas Instruments (TI), which clearly took a decisive lead in the semiconductor industry, refers to the basic conviction of its president that led to TI's signal contribution to semiconductor device utilization in the United States and the world:

During 1949 and 1950 it finally became clear to me that the future of electronics would be profoundly influenced by knowledge already attained and additional knowledge being rapidly gained about materials at the *structure-of-matter level* . . . .In early 1951 we began to formalize our strategy by *definite commitment to develop, manufacture and market semiconductor devices.* [emphasis added][23]

The Market

Convinced that structure-of-matter level developments would determine the most significant marketing opportunities, TI President Haggerty chose a series of strategies to capture them:

Fig. 1.2
Comparable Funding: SDI Comparable National Priority Programs

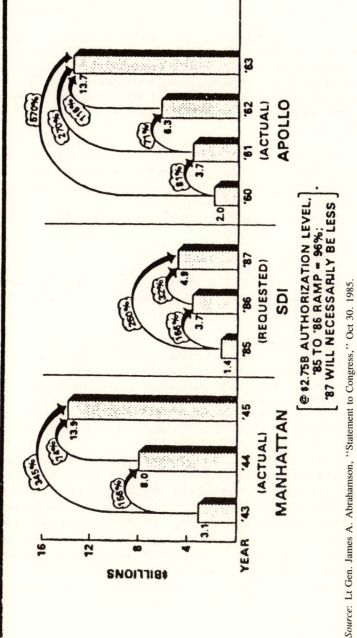

Source: Lt Gen. James A. Abrahamson, "Statement to Congress," Oct 30. 1985.

15

The three principal tactics we used to fulfill our semiconductor strategy were: (1) the development of the first silicon transistor, (2) the development and marketing of the first pocket radio, the famous Regency, in collaboration with the IDEA Corporation, and (3) the development of our process for production of pure silicon . . . .

From this *first semiconductor strategy*, the beginnings of a *second* can be traced to discussions in 1956 between Willis Adcock and me in which *we speculated on* the feasibility of whole circuits processed in minute *wafers* of pure silicon. That dream became a reality with the invention of the *first practical integrated circuit* by Jack Kilby . . . .Jack invented the integrated circuit in the summer of 1958, just ten years after the invention of the transistor by Doctors Brattain and Boredeen of the Bell Telephone Laboratories. [emphasis added][24]

The technological foundation of both the semiconductor strategies lay in the ''firsts'': first silicon transistor, first pocket radio, and the first practical integrated circuit. Being firsts, the management decision to create those firsts was taken clearly when there was no assurance either that the firsts would ever be accomplished or that they would be accomplished first at TI.

The Resources

To catapult 40-fold from $5.8 million in 1949 to $200 million, based on the still unproven semiconductor devices, TI had to commit 100 percent of the next four years' net profits:

The cost of carrying out this strategy for the years 1952 through 1955 was $1,250,000. This was our accumulated loss, including *R&D costs* for the total program, less income generated. In addition, we had committed total assets of about $3,000,000, a large proportion of which would *not* be *salvageable if our strategy failed*. Now $1,250,000 was a *lot of money* for us in those years. This becomes evident by comparison with our total net sales billed of $20,500,000 and net profits after taxes of $900,000 in 1952, or $28,700,000 sales billed and $1,600,000 in profits in 1955. [emphasis added][25]

If ($1.25 + $3.00 =) $4.25 million (probably estimated at $4–5 mill. at the outset) were to be committed at a time when the net sales for the year was $20.5 million, and net profits after taxes only $0.9 million, the investment had better be very compelling! In retrospect, we see that the $4.25-million investment was made during four years when the total sales were $97.4 million, and when the total profit was $4.25, using 1952 figures for 1953 and 1954. In other words 4.37 percent of four years' net sales and 100 percent of four years' net profits were committed to the semiconductor strategy when the silicon semiconductor was a dream.

The Decision

Haggerty was convinced that TI should pursue what he calls a ''breakthrough strategy,'' at very large risks:

If an innovative effort is to be of such significance that, if it succeeds, it really will have a major impact on a big company—a *true breakthrough strategy* (the sort of single strategy, the success of which can produce 10% growth rates per year all by itself, even in a large corporation)—then at some critical time in its development *the risk will be very large*. General management must understand both the risks and the potential rewards.

Case after case can be listed: RCA and color television; IBM and the 360; Xerox, at least twice; Texas Instruments and its early breakthroughs in semiconductors; Boeing and the 707.

If the management doesn't understand, the resources applied simply will not be adequate and the strategy will fail, and *no innovation will result*—not because it wasn't potentially there, but because the management simply *lacked the comprehension and the courage to proceed*. [emphasis supplied][26]

MARKET APPLICATION 2: "YOU BET THE COMPANY"

Haggerty mentions IBM 360 as a true breakthrough strategy.

The Decision

IBM was the market leader in second-generation computers when it decided to "go for broke" on the third generation. It was not to protect the present market, but the potential market, that IBM decided to develop computers incorporating integrated circuits. In the words of J.-J. Servan-Schreiber:

To build the 360, IBM turned its administrative and management structure inside out. Executives who lost the company two years by ignoring the industrial possibilities of integrated circuits were replaced. With a new set of managers, IBM offered fantastic salaries to steal the best technicians it could find from its competitors.[27]

The Market

A whole new market in both hardware and software had to be developed. The dynamic management of storage space by the executive program had to be coupled with the hardware ability to retrieve data efficiently, offering to the customer the prospect of a hardware-software combination. The invention of a brand new programming language, PL/I, underscored this new development. If IBM could be the first to offer third-generation computers, that would ensure IBM's dominance.

The Resources

The risk indeed was large. Servan-Schreiber says that over a four-year period, IBM invested $5 billion. The $5-billion investment should be compared with the approximately $1.5-billion sales a year, or approximately $6-billion sales during the four years, or 83 percent of the sales for the next four years.

The Decision

IBM decided to strike out into the unknown third-generation computer systems in order to survive in the potential market. The outcome was by no means certain at the time of the decision nor during the next four years. General Electric bought out Olivetti in Italy and Bull in France to compete with IBM. The stakes were quite high; the risks were enormous. IBM made the decision, invested the resources, and won.

CONCLUDING OBSERVATIONS

The twin imperatives of technology management are the survival of the country and the survival of the corporation. Hi-tech underpins survival on both fronts. It is not just hi-tech that has assured survival, but more often than not, hi-tech that is years away.

Today, President Reagan's commitment to the Strategic Defense Initiative (SDI) is based on a technological breakthrough which would intercept enemy missiles in space. It will be years before it can be known if the concept is even feasible.

If SDI relates to military missions, Japan's fifth-generation computer systems (5G) relates to markets, both domestic and foreign. The very survival of U.S. markets is seriously threatened by Japan securing the world market for hi-tech yet to be born, illustrated by its securing 90 percent of the world market for 256-kilobit D-RAMS.

What makes for successful betting on unborn hi-tech for survival? We looked at six historic decisions, relating to four missions for country survival and two markets for corporate survival. The British decision to invent radar technology to survive; the U.S. decision to invent atomic technology to survive; the U.S. decision to invent space technology to survive in the international technology arena; and the U.S. decision to invent non-nuclear space defense technology to survive were each briefly analyzed in terms of the decision, the mission, and the resources.

Critical to the survival of the corporation as a preeminent leader in the particular hi-tech area, and equally critical to the survival of the country leadership in that area, were the Texas Instruments decision to invent semiconductor devices and the IBM decision to invent third-generation computers.

How were these hi-tech decisions made? We will examine the identifiable premises of the decisions in the words of the participants and their immediate associates in the second part of this book. Prior to that we need to identify the nature and magnitude of the total resources available to be invested in basic research, applied research, and development. Since country and corporate survival depend on the same research resources, and since one's gain is the other's loss, there is an inherent conflict between the two on R&D resources commitment, to which we turn next.

Country–Corporate Conflict on R&D Resources Commitment

OVERVIEW: A dollar committed to R&D for missions is a dollar denied to R&D for markets, and vice versa. Therefore, the nearly sixfold increase from $20 billion in 1965 to $118.6 billion in 1986 for R&D should be discussed in terms of basic research, applied research, and development, as well as the changing share of corporate and country commitment to each category.

Is not research in support of missions also supportive of markets? No, says the chairman of the President's Commission on Industrial Competitiveness, John A. Young, himself the president of a major defense contractor, Hewlett-Packard. Military research is now so exotic and so slow in reaching fruition that it has little commercial value.

Of the three categories of R&D, development is closest to the industry's heart, because it gets the products to the market. In 1986, the latest year with detailed statistics, industry contributed $59.48 billion, but performed $87.0-billion worth of R&D, 76.6 percent of which was in development. How much support does development require from basic research?

The National Science Foundation (NSF) sponsored a study of ten innovations of high social impact, ranging from heart pacemakers to video tape recorders. Analysis of the 533 significant events showed that basic research dominated the preconception period, and that half of the basic research occurred 30 years prior to the first realization.

We need an empirical measure which connects the different types of research. R&D Measure 1 is the ratio of innovation to invention, the O/V ratio. Other R&D Measures are: (1) monetary measure of basic research; (2) numerical measure of potential inventors; (3) number and cost of potential innovators; (4) degree and discipline of potential inventors; and (5) share of military R&D.

Basic research depends on instruction covering the entire spectrum of activities which prepare researchers for their task. NSF director Erich Bloch advocates a diversion of funds from applied R&D to the universities and the development of multidisciplinary basic science and technology centers. Fewer high school students choose science and engineering; so do doctoral candidates. Foreign-born doctoral candidates concentrate in engineering. This relationship is measured by R&D measure 7 (native-born/foreign-born) applicants to the Graduate Record Examination (GRE) by field and score.

The conflicting demands of R&D for mission versus R&D for markets upon the four million scientists and engineers in the country call for a concept which recognizes it, developed in chapter 3.

R&D FUNDS FOR COUNTRY AND CORPORATE SURVIVAL

The funds committed in 1986 to fulfill the mission of technology management—country survival and corporate survival—were nearly six times what they were in 1965.

Dollar Value and GNP

Total R&D rose from $20.0 billion in 1965 to $118.6 billion in 1986. The former was 2.9 percent of the Gross National Product (GNP) as is the latter. We see from table 2.1 that the percent share declined from 2.9 in 1965 to 2.2 in 1978, and then rose steadily to 2.9 in 1986.

Categories of R&D

Total R&D is made up of basic research, applied research, and development. Basic research is the advancement of scientific knowledge without specific application or commercial objective, while applied research is application of scientific knowledge with specific objective. Development is the use of scientific knowledge to design and/or produce useful products, processes, and/or services. The formal definitions of the concepts by the National Science Foundation (NSF) are as follows:

Research, which is made up of basic and applied, is systematic, intensive study directed toward fuller scientific knowledge of the subject studied.

Basic research. For three of the sectors—Federal Government, universities and colleges, and other nonprofit institutions—the definition of basic research stresses that it is directed toward increases of knowledge in science with ''the primary aim of the investigator . . . a fuller knowledge or understanding of the subject under study, rather than a practical application thereof.'' To take account of an individual industrial company's commercial goals, the definition for the industry sector is modified to indicate that basic research projects represent ''original investigations for the advancement of scientific knowledge . . . which do not have specific commercial objectives, although they may be in fields of present or potential interest to the reporting company.''

Table 2.1
R&D—Total, Components, Federal Funding, 1970–1988 ($ Billions)

R&D	1970	1975	1978	1980	1984	1985	1986	1987	1988
TOTAL R&D	26.1	35.2	48.1	62.6	97.6	107.4	114.7	123.0	131.6
In 1982 $	62.4	59.9	66.8	73.2	90.5	96.5	100.4	104.6	108.2
% of GNP	2.6%	2.3%	2.1%	2.3%	2.6%	2.7%	2.8%	2.8%	2.9%
TOTAL R&D	26.1	35.2	48.1	62.6	97.6	107.4	114.7	123.0	131.6
Research-Basic	13.6%	13.1%	13.3%	12.9%	12.3%	12.2%	12.3%	12.1%	11.8%
Research-Applied	21.9%	22.3%	22.5%	22.4%	22.7%	22.9%	21.6%	21.1%	20.6%
Development	64.5%	64.6%	64.2%	64.7%	65.0%	64.9%	66.1%	66.8%	67.6%
TOTAL R&D	100%	100%	100%	100%	100%	100%	100%	100%	100%
TOTAL R&D	26.1	35.2	48.1	62.6	97.6	107.4	114.7	123.0	131.6
% Federal as Source	57.0%	51.4%	49.6%	47.1%	46.5%	47.7%	48.2%	49.0%	49.0%
RESEARCH - Basic and Applied									
TOTAL	9.3	12.5	17.2	22.1	34.2	37.7	38.9	41.0	42.7
% Federal as Source	60.1%	56.8%	56.1%	54.9%	52.0%	53.0%	51.4%	51.2%	49.9%
RESEARCH - Basic									
Total	3.5	4.6	6.4	8.1	12.0	13.1	14.2	14.9	15.5
% Federal as Source	70.1%	68.1%	69.5%	68.8%	64.9%	64.4%	64.5%	64.7%	63.8%
DEVELOPMENT									
TOTAL	16.9	22.7	30.9	40.4	63.4	69.7	75.8	82.1	88.9
%Federal as Source	55.3%	48.5%	46.0%	42.7%	43.3%	45.0%	46.5%	48.0%	48.6%

Applied research. The core definition in the NSF questionnaire sent to universities and colleges is: "*Applied research* is directed toward practical application of knowledge." Here again, the definition for the industry survey takes account of the characteristics of industrial organizations. It covers "research projects which represent investigations directed to discovery of new scientific knowledge and which have specific commercial objectives with respect to either projects or processes." By this definition, applied research in industry differs from basic research chiefly in terms of objectives of the reporting company.

*Development.*The NSF survey concept of development may be summarized as "the systematic use of scientific knowledge directed toward the production of useful materials, devices, systems or methods, including design and development of prototypes and pro- cesses."[1]

Country Role: Decreasing Federal Share of R&D Funds

In 1965 the federal government was the source of 64.9 percent of R&D funds; in 1975, 51.4 percent; in 1985, 47.2 percent; and in 1986, 46.4 percent.

Corporate Role: Increasing Industry Share of Development

Development has dominated R&D outlay, accounting for 2 out of 3 dollars. In 1965, $13.15 billion for development was 65.6 percent of total R&D; $22.74 billion in 1975 was 64.6 percent; $71.6 billion in 1985 was 65.8 percent; and $78.85 billion in 1986 was 66.5 percent of total R&D.

What are the sources of development funds? We see from table 2.2 that $4.433 billion out of $13.150 billion came from industry, or 33.71 percent. In 1975, industry share rose to 51.00 percent, which further rose to 54.19 percent in 1986, the latest year of detailed statistics.

What share of industry funds was spent for development? In 1965, the total contribution by industry to R&D was $6.548 billion (tab. 2.3), of which $4.433 went to development, or 66.17 percent. In 1975, industry contributed $15.820 billion, 73.33 percent of which went to development. In 1986, 71.84 percent of $59.475 billion went to development.

What share of industry performance was for development? While industry contributed $59.475 billion to R&D in 1986, it performed $87.000 billion worth of R&D, as seen from table 2.4. The $87 billion was made up of $66.6 in development, $17.3 in applied R&D, and $3.1 billion in basic research. In other words, 76.6 percent of industry R&D performance was in development, 19.9 percent in applied research, and 3.3 percent in basic research.

We see that nearly four out of five dollars of industry performance of R&D were devoted to development. Development concentrates on using scientific knowledge to design and/or produce useful products, processes, and/or services. By "useful" is meant usefulness to the market. Since industry criteria are based on profit, and profit is generated by sales, development which produces saleable products is near and dear to industry's heart.

Table 2.2
Sources of Funds for Development by Sector: 1953, 1960, and 1965–1986
($ Millions)

Current dollars

Year	Total	Federal Government	Industry	Universities and colleges	Other nonprofit institutions
1953	3,404	1,755	1,637	5	7
1960	9,306	6,335	2,948	11	12
1965	13,150	8,679	4,433	15	23
1966	14,431	9,408	4,977	18	28
1967	15,310	9,500	5,761	20	29
1968	16,178	9,782	6,345	17	34
1969	16,874	9,669	7,150	17	38
1970	16,865	9,323	7,489	13	40
1971	17,265	9,427	7,781	14	43
1972	18,664	10,071	8,532	19	42
1973	20,175	10,296	9,797	33	49
1974	21,397	10,404	10,895	42	56
1975	22,742	11,030	11,598	47	67
1976	24,995	11,944	12,922	52	77
1977	27,501	12,985	14,369	58	89
1978	30,893	14,202	16,505	78	108
1979	35,304	15,901	19,196	85	122
1980	40,464	17,293	22,951	90	130
1981	45,783	19,720	25,827	101	135
1982	50,861	21,724	28,867	120	150
1983	55,795	24,152	31,352	126	165
1984	62,856	27,669	34,877	130	180
1985 (est.)...	71,575	32,325	38,915	140	195
1986 (est.)...	78,850	35,760	42,730	150	210

Constant dollars[1]

Year	Total	Federal Government	Industry	Universities and colleges	Other nonprofit institutions
1953	13,127	6,758	6,323	19	27
1960	30,049	20,450	9,525	35	39
1965	38,934	25,698	13,123	44	68
1966	41,317	26,949	14,236	52	80
1967	42,601	26,435	16,029	56	81
1968	42,965	26,012	16,817	46	90
1969	42,500	24,387	17,974	43	96
1970	40,206	22,261	17,818	31	95
1971	39,003	21,341	17,533	32	97
1972	40,206	21,722	18,352	41	90
1973	40,878	20,934	19,776	68	99
1974	39,854	19,478	20,191	81	105
1975	38,525	18,775	19,555	82	114
1976	39,719	19,025	20,489	84	122
1977	40,896	19,320	21,357	87	132
1978	42,819	19,707	22,854	109	150
1979	44,986	20,290	24,432	109	156
1980	47,273	20,240	26,775	106	152
1981	48,774	21,034	27,487	108	144
1982	50,861	21,724	28,867	120	150
1983	53,695	23,229	30,187	121	159
1984	58,131	25,578	32,267	120	166
1985 (est.)...	64,029	28,895	34,836	125	174
1986 (est.)...	68,169	30,901	36,957	129	181

[1]Based on GNP implicit price deflator.
SOURCE: National Science Foundation

Table 2.3
Sources of Funds for Research and Development by Sector: 1953, 1960, and 1965–1986 ($ Millions)

Current dollars

Year	Total	Federal Government	Industry	Universities and colleges	Other nonprofit institutions
1953	5,124	2,753	2,245	72	54
1960	13,523	8,738	4,516	149	120
1965	20,044	13,012	6,548	267	217
1966	21,846	13,968	7,328	304	246
1967	23,146	14,395	8,142	345	264
1968	24,605	14,928	9,005	390	282
1969	25,631	14,895	10,010	420	306
1970	26,134	14,892	10,444	461	337
1971	26,676	14,964	10,822	529	361
1972	28,477	15,808	11,710	574	385
1973	30,718	16,399	13,293	613	413
1974	32,864	16,850	14,878	677	459
1975	35,213	18,109	15,820	749	535
1976	39,018	19,914	17,694	810	600
1977	42,783	21,594	19,629	888	672
1978	48,129	23,876	22,450	1,037	766
1979	54,933	26,815	26,081	1,200	837
1980	62,593	29,451	30,911	1,323	908
1981	71,840	33,405	35,944	1,520	971
1982	79,328	36,505	40,096	1,702	1,025
1983	87,178	40,667	43,514	1,864	1,133
1984	97,275	45,249	48,821	2,000	1,205
1985 (est.)..	108,800	50,915	54,385	2,200	1,300
1986 (est.)..	118,600	55,250	59,475	2500	1375

Constant dollars[1]

Year	Total	Federal Government	Industry	Universities and colleges	Other nonprofit institutions
1953	19,744	10,590	8,671	276	208
1960	43,648	28,191	14,591	479	387
1965	59,351	38,532	19,384	791	643
1966	62,589	40,047	20,962	875	706
1967	64,406	40,057	22,654	960	735
1968	65,458	39,788	23,869	1,049	752
1969	64,672	37,660	25,166	1,071	775
1970	62,405	35,636	24,851	1,111	807
1971	60,385	33,966	24,387	1,212	820
1972	61,414	34,146	25,190	1,246	832
1973	62,427	33,478	26,837	1,268	844
1974	61,467	31,726	27,578	1,298	865
1975	59,883	30,986	26,679	1,302	916
1976	62,134	31,813	28,058	1,305	959
1977	63,653	32,152	29,176	1,325	1,001
1978	66,769	33,172	31,087	1,446	1,064
1979	70,077	34,271	33,197	1,540	1,069
1980	73,235	34,546	36,064	1,561	1,065
1981	76,610	35,685	38,257	1,631	1,037
1982	79,328	36,505	40,096	1,702	1,025
1983	83,862	39,090	41,895	1,788	1,089
1984	89,937	41,813	45,166	1,845	1,113
1985 (est.)..	97,283	45,481	48,682	1,960	1,161
1986 (est.)..	102,504	47,722	51,438	2,156	1,187

[1]Based on GNP implicit price deflator.
SOURCE: National Science Foundation

Table 2.4
Research and Development Performance by Sector: 1953, 1960, and 1965–1986
($ Millions)

Current dollars

Year	Total	Federal Government	Industry	Universities and colleges	Associated FFRDC's	Other nonprofit institutions
1953	5,124	1,010	3,630	255	121	108
1960	13,523	1,726	10,509	646	360	282
1965	20,044	3,093	14,185	1,474	629	663
1966	21,846	3,220	15,548	1,715	630	733
1967	23,146	3,396	16,385	1,921	673	771
1968	24,605	3,494	17,429	2,149	719	814
1969	25,631	3,503	18,308	2,225	725	870
1970	26,134	4,079	18,067	2,335	737	916
1971	26,676	4,228	18,320	2,500	716	912
1972	28,477	4,590	19,552	2,630	753	952
1973	30,718	4,762	21,249	2,884	817	1,006
1974	32,864	4,911	22,887	3,023	865	1,178
1975	35,213	5,354	24,187	3,409	987	1,276
1976	39,018	5,769	26,997	3,729	1,147	1,376
1977	42,783	6,012	29,825	4,067	1,384	1,495
1978	48,129	6,811	33,304	4,625	1,717	1,672
1979	54,933	7,417	38,226	5,361	1,935	1,994
1980	62,593	7,632	44,505	6,060	2,246	2,150
1981	71,840	8,425	51,810	6,819	2,486	2,300
1982	79,328	9,141	57,995	7,288	2,479	2,425
1983	87,178	10,582	63,403	7,781	2,737	2,675
1984	97,275	11,572	71,137	8,473	3,118	2,975
1985 (est.) .	108,800	13,150	79,500	9,500	3,400	3,250
1986 (est) . .	118,600	14,000	87,000	10,600	3,600	3,400

Constant dollars[1]

Year	Total	Federal Government	Industry	Universities and colleges	Associated FFRDC's	Other nonprofit institutions
1953	19,744	3,867	14,021	976	463	417
1960	43,648	5,548	33,955	2,077	1,157	911
1965	59,351	9,164	41,992	4,367	1,864	1,963
1966	62,589	9,269	44,474	4,937	1,813	2,097
1967	64,406	9,452	45,590	5,347	1,873	2,145
1968	65,458	9,395	46,194	5,778	1,933	2,157
1969	64,672	8,936	46,023	5,676	1,849	2,187
1970	62,405	9,834	42,986	5,629	1,777	2,179
1971	60,385	9,684	41,280	5,726	1,640	2,055
1972	61,414	9,965	42,056	5,710	1,635	2,048
1973	62,427	9,849	42,893	5,965	1,690	2,031
1974	61,467	9,415	42,415	5,796	1,658	2,183
1975	59,883	9,308	40,781	5,927	1,716	2,151
1976	62,134	9,293	42,805	6,007	1,848	2,182
1977	63,653	8,969	44,330	6,067	2,065	2,222
1978	66,769	9,497	46,115	6,449	2,394	2,315
1979	70,077	9,521	48,652	6,882	2,484	2,538
1980	73,235	9,006	51,919	7,151	2,650	2,508
1981	76,610	9,039	55,140	7,316	2,667	2,448
1982	79,328	9,141·	57,995	7,288	2,479	2,425
1983	83,862	10,151	61,047	7,464	2,625	2,576
1984	89,937	10,677	65,813	7,818	2,877	2,752
1985 (est.) .	97,283	11,715	71,166	8,463	3,029	2,909
1986 (est) . .	102,504	12,072	75,246	9,140	3,104	2,941

[1]Based on GNP implicit price deflator.
SOURCE: National Science Foundation

INSTRUCTION, INVENTION, AND INNOVATION

Development makes a product (process) marketable (*innovation*). It is the output for which the input is a new idea (*invention*). An ounce of invention often requires a ton of *instruction*.

An Analogy

Of the triad, innovation is the most visible because it is the embodiment of an invention in a marketable product or process. If we compare innovation to the fruit, invention is the flower. The least visible of the triad is instruction, under which term we include not only educational instruction, but also the extensive preparations needed to equip the few to perform basic research, applied research, and development. In terms of our fruit and flower analogy, instruction is the plant itself.

If we keep looking only for the fruit, most human effort essential to eventual fruition—the long and toilsome preparation of the soil, the planting of the seed, the watering of the soil, the protection of the plant from insects, and the fertilizing of the plant—would appear irrelevant and unproductive, because none of the activities immediately yield fruit. By the same token, the sprouting of the plant, the growing of the stem, the sprouting of the leaf buds, the growing of the stem and of the branches, the sprouting of the flower buds and the blossoms, and the pollination of the flowers would all appear superfluous to immediate interest in the fruit.

Definition of Innovation, Invention, and Instruction

Innovation is the modification of an invention to meet a present and/or potential demand. *Invention* is a new concept, process, and/or product which explains phenomena and/or performs functions more elegantly and/or effectively. *Instruction* is the imparting of operational knowledge of subject matter and research methods to stimulate sustained independent effort.

INVENTION AND INNOVATION

We define *trade drain* as the imbalance among the triad elements—instruction, invention, and innovation. No one country can excel in all three all the time. Roughly speaking, Japan excels in innovation, and the United States in invention. Japan's careful cultivation of world markets—innovation—builds up her trade surplus. Her trade surplus with the United States was $35 billion in 1985, the first year in three generations that the United States became a net debtor to the world; and the surplus has been steadily mounting.

How can the United States and Japan manage the trade drain to their mutual advantage? We will develop a new concept which provides an analytical framework in the next chapter. In this chapter, we will develop the principal elements of R&D and their measures.

Basic Research Input

Basic research, which produces invention, appears remote to the development, which produces innovation. Even more remote is the wellspring of invention, instruction. If basic research is ignored, how long will it be before adverse results appear in development?

NSF study of ten innovations, ranging from oral contraceptives to video tape recorders, and from hybrid corn to input-output analysis, offers some specific guidelines.

NSF Study—Selection of Ten Innovations

In 1968 NSF funded a study by the Illinois Institute of Technology titled "Technology in Retrospect and Critical Events in Science" (TRACES). Five years later, three cases of "socially desirable" innovation from the project and five new cases (which represented seven distinct innovations) were studied by Battelle Columbus Laboratories, refining the TRACES methodology. The Battelle project team and NSF selected ten innovations of "high social impact" in "diverse fields of technology and application": (1) the heart pacemaker, (2) hybrid grains and the green revolution, (3) electrophotography, (4) input-output economic analysis, (5) organophosphorus insecticides, (6) oral contraceptives, (7) magnetic ferrites, and (8) video tape recorders.

Inventions and "Decisive" Events

The Battelle study refines the TRACES concept of "event":

The innovative process comprises myriad occurrences, some of which happen sequentially, and some concurrently at different places. From these occurrences, one can identify some that appear to encapsulate the progress of the innovation. These special occurrences are the "events" in the technical sense just referred to. Their selection reflects the best judgment of the investigators, and is necessarily somewhat arbitrary . . . .

A *decisive event* is an especially important significant event that provides a major and essential impetus to the innovation. It often occurs at the convergence of several streams of activity. In judging an event to be decisive, one should be convinced that, without it, the innovation would not have occurred or would have been seriously delayed.[2]

The study investigated 533 significant events. These were grouped into two research categories—mission-oriented and nonmission-oriented research (MOR and NMOR, respectively), and one category of development:

Nonmission-oriented research (NMOR) is research carried on for the purpose of acquiring new knowledge, according to the conceptual structure of the subject or the interests of the scientist, without concern for a mission application.

Mission-oriented research (MOR) is research carried out for the purpose of acquiring new knowledge expected to be useful in some application.

Development is the process of design, improvement, testing, and engineering, in the course of bringing an innovation to fruition.[3]

The Battelle study terms correspond to the NSF R&D categories:

NMOR	Basic Research (34% of 533 significant events)
MOR	Applied Research (38% of 533 significant events)
Development	Development (26% of 533 significant events)

The Criticality of NMOR

The duration of the innovative process for the 10 innovations ranged from 32 years for the heart pacemaker to 6 years for video tape recorders, the average being 19.2 years (see fig. 2.1).

The distribution of significant events shows that NMOR dominated the pre-conception period (57 percent). During the innovative period, NMOR events were 16 percent, and during the post innovative period, 10 percent.

Figure 2.2 presents the rates of accumulation of NMOR, MOR, and development events:

The events for each innovation have been related in time to the date of first realization of the innovation, and combined and plotted in terms of the number of years prior to that date. The figure indicates that *half of the NMOR occurred 30 years before first realization.* Thus, the innovations made use of published fundamental research which had been available for some time prior to the innovative period. Approximately half of the MOR events occurred in the last 15 years, and approximately half of the developmental activity occurred in the last 10 years.[emphasis added][4]

Basic research tends to be virtually invisible, since its contribution—invention—occurs 30 years prior to the marketable product. "Out of sight, out of mind" is a rule too readily applied to basic research funding. Instruction fares even worse.

COUNTRY AND CORPORATE INVESTMENT IN BASIC RESEARCH

We will look at the dollar value of country and corporate investment in basic research, applied research, and their relationship.

Fig. 2.1
Distribution of Significant Events in the Preconception, Innovative, and Postinnovative Periods

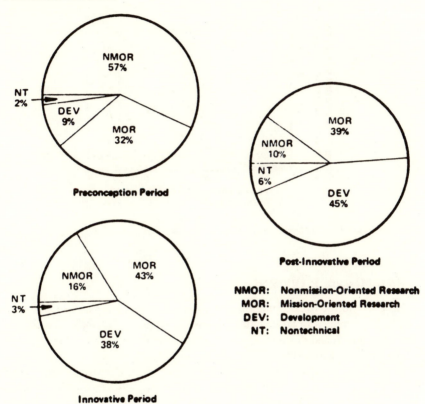

Source: National Science Foundation

Monetary Measure of Basic and Applied Research

In 1986 industry provided $2.995 billion, 20.73 percent of the total $14.45 billion spent on basic research, while the federal government provided 63.94 percent. Universities and colleges provided 10.59 percent, and other nonprofit institutions 4.74 percent (tab. 2.5).

In 1975, industry provided 15.30 percent, and in 1965, 18.04 percent. The corresponding figures for the federal government were 68.12 percent in 1975, and 70.72 percent in 1965.

How much did the one-seventh to one-fifth of basic research mean to industry? In 1965, basic research represented 7.04 percent of industry's outlay on R&D; in 1975, 4.46 percent; and in 1986, 5.01 percent.

During the same period, the basic research share of the federal government R&D rose from 13.90 percent in 1965 to 16.72 percent in 1986.

Technology Management

Fig. 2.2
Cumulative Increase in Types of Significant Events

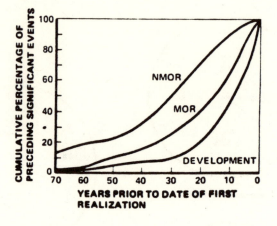

Source: National Science Foundation

R&D Measure 1: O/V Ratio

How should the R&D dollar be best allocated between basic or nonmission-oriented research, with no specified commercial objective, on the one hand, and applied research and development, or mission-oriented research, with specified commercial objective(s)?

If we treat "applied research and development" as "innovation," and "basic research" as "invention," we define the ratio of innovation/invention as the O/V ratio, the *O* signifying inn*O*vation, and the *V* signifying in*V*ention. Table 2.6 presents the O/V ratio for 1965–1986. Basic research is supporting an increasing value of applied R&D over the 20 years, rising from 6.84 in 1965 to 7.21 in 1986.

In other words, the basic research dollar has had to support 5.4 percent more of applied research and development in 1986 than it did in 1965. This heavier burden placed on basic research will show itself over the long term. How critical is basic research to invention?

R&D INFRASTRUCTURE

To make invention possible, an extensive support structure is essential. In terms of our analogy, it requires not only pollinating the flower, but also nurturing a plant from seed to flowering. We may start our study of the process with the exploration of the quantitative and nominal indices of infrastructure.

Table 2.5
Sources of Funds for Basic Research by Sector: 1953, 1960, and 1965–1986
($ Millions)

Current dollars

Year	Total	Federal Government	Industry	Universities and colleges	Other nonprofit institutions
1953	441	251	153	10	27
1960	1,197	715	342	72	68
1965	2,555	1,809	461	164	121
1966	2,814	1,978	510	197	129
1967	3,056	2,201	492	223	140
1968	3,296	2,336	535	276	149
1969	3,441	2,441	540	298	162
1970	3,549	2,489	528	350	182
1971	3,672	2,529	547	400	196
1972	3,829	2,633	563	415	218
1973	3,946	2,709	605	408	224
1974	4,239	2,912	651	432	244
1975	4,608	3,139	705	478	286
1976	4,977	3,436	769	475	297
1977	5,537	3,823	850	527	337
1978	6,392	4,445	964	605	378
1979	7,257	5,044	1,091	711	411
1980	8,079	5,559	1,265	805	450
1981	9,180	6,211	1,588	906	475
1982	9,947	6,646	1,813	992	496
1983	11,028	7,269	2,059	1,125	575
1984	12,123	7,896	2,439	1,203	585
1985 (est.)...	13,325	8,645	2,745	1,290	645
1986 (est.)...	14,450	9,240	2,995	1,530	685

Constant dollars[1]

Year	Total	Federal Government	Industry	Universities and colleges	Other nonprofit institutions
1953	1,695	962	591	38	104
1960	3,856	2,301	1,105	231	219
1965	7,568	5,359	1,365	486	358
1966	8,084	5,687	1,459	567	370
1967	8,505	6,125	1,369	621	390
1968	8,826	6,267	1,419	742	398
1969	8,744	6,214	1,359	760	411
1970	8,527	5,990	1,278	844	436
1971	8,377	5,780	1,234	916	446
1972	8,294	5,710	1,212	901	472
1973	8,112	5,586	1,224	844	459
1974	8,056	5,557	1,210	828	461
1975	7,951	5,436	1,192	831	491
1976	7,985	5,523	1,221	765	475
1977	8,253	5,701	1,264	786	502
1978	8,897	6,192	1,336	844	525
1979	9,296	6,468	1,390	913	525
1980	9,506	6,550	1,478	950	528
1981	9,828	6,657	1,692	972	508
1982	9,947	6,646	1,813	992	496
1983	10,590	6,976	1,982	1,079	552
1984	11,195	7,288	2,256	1,110	540
1985 (est.)...	11,888	7,707	2,456	1,149	576
1986 (est.)...	12,471	7,971	2,589	1,319	591

[1]Based on GNP implicit price deflator.
SOURCE: National Science Foundation

Table 2.6
O/V Ratio, 1965–1988

Year	Total R&D	Basic Research	% Basic Research	% Non-Basic Research	(O/V) Ratio
1965	20,044	2,555	12.75%	87.25%	6.85
1970	26,134	3,549	13.58%	86.42%	6.36
1975	35,213	4,608	13.09%	86.91%	6.64
1980	62,593	8,079	12.91%	87.09%	6.75
1981	71,840	9,180	12.78%	87.22%	6.83
1982	79,328	9,947	12.54%	87.46%	6.98
1983	87,178	11,028	12.65%	87.35%	6.91
1984	96,525	12,123	12.56%	87.44%	6.96
1985	108,800	13,325	12.25%	87.75%	7.17
1986	118,600	14,450	12.18%	87.82%	7.21
1987	123,050	14,950	12.15%	87.85%	7.23
1988	131,600	15,475	11.76%	88.24%	7.50

Basic Source: National Science Foundation

R&D Measure 2: Monetary Measure of Basic Research

The word *infrastructure* is often associated with hi-tech products and processes. Just as it is unreasonable to expect a fruit plucked from a tree and planted elsewhere to take root, grow into a plant, and produce flowers and fruits on its own, so also transplanted hi-tech innovations require sustained support to survive. The word *infra* means "under," as in the arches under a bridge which support the heavy traffic over the bridge. The strength of the superstructure is indeed the strength of the infrastructure, even as the strength of the foundation is the strength of the skyscraper. Without a strong foundation, the skyscraper would collapse.

The infrastructure of "applied research and development" is "basic research." The investment in basic research itself rose from $2.555 billion in 1965 to $14.450 billion in 1986.

R&D Measure 3: Numerical Measure of Potential Inventors

The monetary measure is a surrogate of the "basic research" infrastructure. Money does not invent; people do.

What has the monetary measure represented over the years? The number of "basic research" personnel is hard to come by; so also the number of "R&D" personnel. Therefore, we will consider "R&D" personnel as a whole. Applying the 12 to 13 percent of R&D devoted to basic research, the number of those engaged in basic research can be estimated.

Table 2.7 presents the number of full-time equivalent number of scientists and engineers (S&E) employed. About 70 to 74 percent are employed in industry, while 10 to 12 percent are employed by institutions of higher education. If we consider the scientists and engineers employed in "university-associated federally funded R&D centers" and "other nonprofit institutions" as being engaged in "basic research", we get 45,200 out of a total of 790,000, or 5.7 percent. If we add to that figure half of the S&E in institutions of higher education, we increase the original figure of S&E by 46,650 for a total full-time equivalent S&E in "basic research" of 91,850, or 11.63 percent. It is close to 12.18 percent, which is the ratio of $14.45 billion basic research to total R&D of $118.6 billion.

R&D Measure 4: Number and Cost of Potential Inventors by Industry

By and large, the S&E in industry may be considered as innovators who seek to embody basic research results in marketable products. Admittedly, this is an oversimplification because we do have S&E engaged in basic research in industry. The simplification is similar to our considering half the S&E in institutions of higher learning as engaged in basic research.

Table 2.8 presents the average full-time equivalents (FTE) employment of S&E by industry. Electrical equipment industry, with 121,500 S&E accounts for 21.30 percent of the total, followed by aircraft and missiles industry employing 108,400 and accounting for 19.00 percent.

We see from table 2.9 that the highest average cost per S&E is $227,500 in the motor vehicles industry, followed by $167,600 in aircraft and missiles, the average for all industries being $137,000. The cost in the chemicals industry is below average at $125,200.

R&D Measure 5: Degree and Discipline of Potential Inventors

In table 2.10 we present the characteristics of S&E. Of the 4,246,500 S&E, 4.4 percent is not in the labor force, leaving only 4.060 million available for innovation activities—1.82 million scientists and 2.24 million engineers. The male to female ratio is 86.9 to 13.1.

Table 2.7

Full-time-Equivalent (FTE) Scientists and Engineers Employed in Research and Development by Sector: Selected Years[1] (Thousands)

Sector	1954	1961	1965	1969	1972	1975	1978	1980	1981	1982	1983	1984[2]	1985[2]
Total	237.1	425.7	494.6	553.2	515.3	527.7	587.0	651.7	683.7	702.8	722.9	750.7	790.0
Federal Government[3]	37.7	51.1	61.8	66.5	61.4	58.4	57.1	58.6	59.2	60.0	61.3	61.5	61.5
Industry[4,5]	164.1	312.0	348.4	385.6	353.9	363.8	414.2	469.2	498.8	516.0	533.3	557.4	590.0
Universities and colleges, total	25.0	42.4	53.4	68.3	66.5	69.8	76.6	81.2	83.3	84.4	85.5	88.6	93.3
Scientists and engineers	20.3	33.6	40.4	50.4	48.9	51.2	56.0	57.9	58.9	59.5	60.6	62.5	65.8
Graduate students[6]	4.7	8.8	13.0	17.9	17.6	18.6	20.6	23.3	24.4	24.9	24.9	26.1	27.5
University-associated FFRDC's, total	5.0	9.1	11.1	11.6	11.7	12.7	14.1	15.2	15.4	15.4	15.3	15.2	15.7
Scientists and engineers[6]	4.9	8.8	10.7	11.1	11.3	12.3	13.7	14.8	15.0	15.0	14.9	14.8	15.3
Graduate students[6]	.1	.3	.4	.5	.4	.4	.4	.4	.4	.4	.4	.4	.4
Other nonprofit institutions[4]	5.3	11.1	19.9	21.2	21.8	23.0	25.0	27.5	27.0	27.0	27.5	28.0	29.5

[1]Number of full-time employees plus the FTE of part-time employees. Excludes scientists and engineers employed in State and local government agencies. Totals may be understated by about 5 percent because of incomplete data on summer employment at universities and colleges.

[2]Estimate.

[3]Includes both civilian and military service personnel and managers of R&D.

[4]Includes professional R&D personnel employed at FFRDC's administered by organization in the sector.

[5]Excludes social scientists.

[6]Numbers of FTE graduate students receiving stipends and engaged in R&D.

NOTE: The figures for the industry sector represent yearly averages and may differ from other data in the text which are based upon surveys reporting the employment in a single month of the year.

SOURCE: National Science Foundation

Table 2.8

Full-time Equivalent Number of R&D Scientists and Engineers by Industry: January 1974–1985 (Thousands)

Industry and size of company	SIC code	January											
		1974	1975	1976	1977	1978	1979	1980	1981	1982	1983	1984	1985
Total		360.0	363.3	364.4	382.8	404.4	423.9	450.6	487.8	509.8	522.1	544.5	570.3
Distribution by Industry													
Food and kindred products	20	6.4	6.8	6.9	6.9	6.9	7.4	7.2	7.4	7.4	7.8	7.6	7.9
Textiles and apparel	22,23	1.8	1.8	1.8	1.7	1.8	1.8	(¹)	2.0	1.9	2.0	2.0	2.0
Lumber, wood products, and furniture	24,25	2.1	2.3	2.1	2.1	2.0	1.8	1.7	1.6	(¹)	1.8	(¹)	(¹)
Paper and allied products	26	4.9	5.0	5.2	6.3	6.5	7.1	7.4	8.0	8.4	8.3	7.9	8.2
Chemicals and allied products	28	41.8	45.2	44.4	46.4	48.3	50.0	51.4	54.7	61.6	66.0	67.1	66.9
Industrial chemicals	281-82,286	19.1	21.1	20.1	20.6	21.3	21.4	20.9	21.6	25.9	27.2	26.7	25.1
Drugs and medicines	283	14.0	15.6	16.6	17.8	19.5	20.8	21.6	23.3	25.6	28.2	(¹)	(¹)
Other chemicals	284-84,287-89	8.7	8.5	7.8	8.0	7.5	7.8	8.9	9.8	10.1	10.6	10.3	10.9
Petroleum refining and related industries	29	8.2	8.4	8.6	8.9	9.9	10.1	10.8	13.0	15.6	14.7	13.2	13.4
Rubber products	30	7.7	8.4	8.6	9.1	7.9	8.1	(¹)	10.3	8.1	(¹)	(¹)	(¹)
Stone, clay, and glass products	32	4.5	4.5	4.6	4.5	5.1	5.2	5.4	5.6	5.1	5.0	4.6	5.2
Primary metals	33	6.4	6.3	8.1	8.4	8.1	7.9	8.1	7.9	8.4	8.4	8.5	7.5
Ferrous metals and products	331-32,3398-99	3.3	3.3	3.9	3.9	4.2	4.3	4.7	4.8	5.2	5.3	5.2	4.4
Nonferrous metals and products	333-36	3.1	3.0	4.2	4.5	3.9	3.6	3.4	3.1	3.2	3.1	3.3	3.1
Fabricated metal products	34	7.3	7.4	6.8	7.1	7.0	6.8	7.8	7.8	8.2	(¹)	12.9	(¹)
Machinery	35	51.0	52.8	55.7	55.3	57.8	60.2	62.1	69.2	76.0	76.3	75.0	77.5
Office, computing, and accounting machines	357	34.5	36.1	38.1	37.7	38.9	40.9	41.8	43.7	48.1	49.6	50.3	(¹)
Other machinery, except electrical	351-56,358-59	(¹)	(¹)	(¹)	(¹)	18.9	19.3	20.3	25.5	27.9	26.7	24.7	25.2

Table 2.8 (continued)

Industry and size of company	SIC code	January											
		1974	1975	1976	1977	1978	1979	1980	1981	1982	1983	1984	1985
Electrical equipment	36	82.6	82.6	80.3	84.1	84.4	85.0	94.5	106.9	109.8	110.3	116.1	121.5
Radio and TV receiving equipment	365	1.3	1.0	1.1	.9	1.5	2.1	4.0	7.9	7.8	(¹)	(¹)	(¹)
Communication equipment	366	42.0	40.2	37.4	38.0	39.0	40.4	42.4	44.2	45.9	47.3	56.1	56.8
Electronic components	367	9.6	10.6	10.2	13.0	14.2	14.0	18.1	22.8	24.4	24.5	(¹)	26.5
Other electrical equipment	361-64,369	29.7	30.8	31.6	32.2	29.7	28.5	30.0	32.0	31.7	(¹)	27.9	29.5
Motor vehicles and motor vehicles equipment	371	27.4	26.0	25.4	28.2	31.9	35.2	38.2	35.1	30.0	29.0	28.6	29.1
Other transportation equipment	373-75,379	1.8	1.9	1.7	1.9	1.9	2.0	1.5	1.4	1.2	1.9	(¹)	(¹)
Aircraft and missiles	372,376	70.6	67.5	66.9	72.0	82.0	86.5	85.9	95.2	91.1	95.5	96.5	108.4
Professional and scientific instruments	38	17.5	17.9	18.8	20.5	23.3	27.0	32.8	34.7	42.7	(¹)	(¹)	(¹)
Scientific and mechanical measuring instruments	381-82	5.6	5.9	6.7	7.2	9.0	11.7	(¹)	18.6	(¹)	(¹)	(¹)	(¹)
Optical, surgical, photographic, and other instruments	383-87	11.9	12.0	12.1	13.3	14.3	15.3	16.3	16.0	16.1	(¹)	(¹)	(¹)
Other manufacturing industries	21,27,31,39	3.7	3.7	4.2	4.5	4.6	4.7	4.6	4.8	5.5	6.1	(¹)	(¹)
Nonmanufacturing industries	07-17,41-67,737,739,807,891	14.4	14.9	14.6	15.3	15.0	17.1	19.8	22.2	27.1	26.2	34.9	36.4
Distribution by size of company (based on number of employees)													
Less than 1,000		28.0	30.1	30.2	31.1	29.5	30.5	34.4	38.0	40.7	42.6	53.2	53.2
1,000 to 4,999		28.8	29.9	29.3	28.9	27.5	30.9	34.8	38.9	42.8	44.6	44.8	47.7
5,000 to 9,999		26.4	27.4	26.1	28.6	28.7	30.7	29.6	27.2	36.6	29.5	29.7	32.8
10,000 to 24,999		45.9	47.4	50.6	49.3	52.1	55.6	64.4	71.8	77.0	83.6	82.6	85.1
25,000 or more		230.9	228.5	228.2	244.9	266.6	276.2	287.4	311.8	312.7	321.7	334.2	351.5

¹Not separately available but included in total.
²Data not tabulated at this level prior to the 1977 survey.
SOURCE: National Science Foundation

Table 2.9
Cost per R&D Scientist or Engineer ($ Thousands)

Industry	1970	1975	1980	1981	1982	1983	1984	1985
ALL	48.1	68.5	94.9	103.9	112.4	118.9	129.7	137.0
Chemicals...	42.8	60.9	87.4	96.7	104.4	109.6	119.1	125.2
Machinery...	40.7	58.9	89.9	93.9	102.9	110.9	126.3	136.4
Electrical Equipment...	43.9	62.7	91.1	95.3	105.8	123.2	134.8	146.2
Motor Vehicles....	59.3	88.4	134.3	146.6	162.9	173.8	211.6	227.5
Aircraft & Missiles....	61.3	85.1	101.6	128.4	146.4	144.3	158.4	167.6
Other Industries..	42.4	56.7	86.6	91.3	93.4	96.5	99.6	n.a.

Basic Source: National Science Foundation. The latest annual survey of R&D by Industry available in Spring, 1988 is that for the year 1985.

DEFENSE DOMINANCE OF RESEARCH RESOURCES

The four million scientists and engineers are the fountain-spring of R&D for missions and markets. In general, the larger the share of R&D resources for one activity, missions, the smaller the share for the other activity, markets.

When countries and corporations bet on survival through technological break-throughs, the bottom line is the creativity of their scientific and technological manpower.

The Defense Share of Research Talent

The *Washington Post* says that the U.S. defense establishment has absorbed between *one-third and one-half* of the nation's scientific talent since the Cold War began. [emphasis added][5] Currently, one in three of the new engineer graduates from the Massachusetts Institute of Technology will begin designing weapons.

Missions Versus Markets

Is research research, whether it is done for missions or for markets? Apparently not. There are major differences in terms of objectives, outlook, and approach. The missions R&D is a different breed, as it were, from the markets R&D.

Table 2.10
Scientists and Engineers by Field, Sex, and Labor Force Status: 1976, 1982, and 1984

Field and sex	Total			Labor force			Outside labor force		
	1976	1982	1984	1976	1982	1984	1976	1982	1984
Total, all fields	2,523,600	3,506,000	4,246,500	2,369,000	3,327,200	4,060,500	154,600	178,800	186,000
Men	2,270,600	3,068,800	3,683,500	2,148,500	2,919,800	3,529,800	122,100	149,000	153,700
Women	253,000	437,200	536,000	220,500	407,400	530,800	32,500	29,800	32,300
Total scientists	1,256,900	1,519,000	1,895,000	1,177,700	1,444,200	1,819,100	79,200	75,100	75,900
Men	1,016,800	1,147,200	1,412,900	968,800	1,097,800	1,365,100	48,000	49,400	47,900
Women	240,100	372,100	482,000	208,900	346,300	454,000	31,200	25,700	28,000
Physical scientists	223,600	249,400	273,700	200,700	233,200	258,800	22,900	16,300	14,900
Men	196,300	223,100	241,800	178,500	209,700	229,400	17,800	13,400	12,400
Women	27,300	26,400	31,900	22,200	23,500	29,400	5,100	2,900	2,500
Mathematical scientists	96,000	86,300	107,500	90,200	81,100	102,600	5,800	5,200	4,900
Men	79,700	57,900	83,200	76,200	55,000	80,100	3,500	3,000	3,100
Women	16,300	28,300	24,300	14,000	26,100	22,500	2,300	2,200	1,800
Computer specialists	209,500	309,100	444,600	204,100	302,200	439,300	5,400	6,900	5,300
Men	171,900	224,900	326,300	169,900	222,400	324,200	2,100	2,400	2,100
Women	37,600	84,300	118,300	34,200	79,700	115,100	3,400	4,500	3,200
Environmental scientists	70,800	95,300	105,600	66,300	89,800	101,200	4,600	5,500	4,400
Men	65,600	81,100	93,600	61,900	76,700	90,100	3,700	4,400	3,500
Women	5,300	14,200	12,000	4,300	13,100	11,100	900	1,100	900
Life scientists	298,300	365,500	383,700	282,900	345,500	361,100	15,400	20,000	22,600
Men	242,700	286,900	288,700	234,500	273,200	274,800	8,100	13,700	13,900
Women	55,600	78,600	95,000	48,300	72,300	86,400	7,300	6,300	8,700
Psychologists	118,200	149,400	223,100	112,300	142,900	214,900	5,900	6,500	8,200
Men	79,700	88,300	127,400	75,800	85,400	123,700	2,100	2,900	3,800
Women	40,300	61,100	95,600	36,600	56,500	91,300	3,800	3,600	4,400
Social scientists	240,500	264,300	356,900	221,300	249,500	341,200	19,100	14,700	15,700
Men	182,600	185,000	252,000	172,000	175,400	242,900	10,700	9,600	9,100
Women	57,800	79,300	104,900	49,400	74,100	98,200	8,500	5,100	6,700

	C1	C2	C3	C4	C5	C6	C7	C8	C9
Total engineers	110,100	103,700	75,400	2,241,400	1,883,000	1,191,300	2,351,500	1,986,700	1,266,700
Men	105,800	99,600	24,100	2,164,700	1,821,900	1,179,700	2,270,600	1,921,600	1,253,800
Women	4,300	4,100	1,300	76,700	61,000	11,600	80,900	65,100	12,900
Aeronautical/astronautical	4,800	4,700	1,400	97,700	82,300	39,700	102,600	87,100	41,400
Men	4,500	4,700	1,100	95,500	80,100	39,100	100,000	84,800	40,200
Women	300	(¹)	300	2,200	2,200	600	2,600	2,200	900
Chemical	13,000	8,500	2,800	143,500	111,000	60,700	156,600	119,500	63,500
Men	12,000	7,500	2,700	134,200	104,500	59,100	146,300	112,000	61,800
Women	1,000	1,000	100	9,300	6,500	1,600	10,300	7,500	1,700
Civil	21,800	14,200	6,500	317,900	263,400	154,100	339,700	277,600	160,600
Men	21,400	13,700	6,500	308,200	257,000	152,200	329,500	270,600	158,700
Women	400	500	(¹)	9,700	6,500	1,900	10,100	6,900	1,900
Electrical/electronics	24,400	19,100	4,900	505,300	443,100	196,900	529,700	462,200	201,700
Men	23,200	18,500	4,400	493,000	433,500	196,100	516,200	452,000	200,500
Women	1,100	600	400	12,300	9,600	800	13,500	10,200	1,200
Industrial	3,400	7,200	(²)	133,400	115,900	(²)	136,800	123,100	(²)
Men	3,200	6,800	(²)	127,800	111,100	(²)	131,100	117,900	(²)
Women	200	300	(²)	5,500	4,800	(²)	5,700	5,200	(²)
Materials	2,400	2,800	(²)	52,300	40,200	(²)	54,700	43,000	(²)
Men	2,300	2,700	(²)	49,900	38,200	(²)	52,200	40,900	(²)
Women	100	100	(²)	2,400	2,000	(²)	2,500	2,100	(²)
Mechanical	31,300	23,300	4,100	452,100	365,500	207,400	483,300	388,700	211,600
Men	30,600	22,900	4,100	440,600	357,900	206,200	471,200	380,900	210,300
Women	700	400	(¹)	11,500	7,400	1,200	12,100	7,900	1,300
Other[3]	9,000	23,900	55,700	539,300	461,800	532,500	548,200	485,600	588,200
Men	8,500	22,800	55,300	515,500	439,600	527,000	524,000	462,400	582,300
Women	500	1,100	400	23,800	22,200	5,500	24,200	23,200	5,900

[1]Too few cases to estimate.
[2]Data unavailable.
[3]In 1976, "other" includes industrial and materials engineering.
NOTE: Detail may not add to totals because of rounding.
SOURCE: National Science Foundation

The chairman of the President's Commission on Industrial Competitiveness, John A. Young, himself the president of a major defense contractor, Hewlett-Packard, emphasizes that military research is now so exotic, and so slow in reaching fruition, that it has little commercial use.[6]

Not only does missions research *not* offer results immediately transferable to markets, but also it generates an outlook and approach which are counterproductive in the marketplace. In the words of Theodore Williams, chairman and chief executive officer of Bell Industries, Inc., a hi-tech firm in Los Angeles employing two thousand, "It is impossible to mix defense business with commercial or industrial business. Engineers tend to *overdesign, without concern for cost.* . . . In the commercial sector, if you bring that mentality into it, people couldn't afford to buy anything." [emphasis added][7]

Cutting Edge in Defense, Undercutting in Commerce

The concentration of U.S. scientific and engineering talent on defense since 1950 when President Truman authorized the work leading to the first hydrogen bomb, has certainly forged the cutting edge of U.S. defense technology. And, under the terms of the surrender of Germany and Japan, neither nation could develop significant military forces of their own. Instead, they were to rely on the United States to defend them. This enabled them to concentrate their resources on commercial enterprises.

While the gainful employment of scientific and engineering personnel of his electoral district is most welcome to any congressman, Representative Mel Levine (Democrat from California) whose district depends on defense is worried: "While we're building technology on the cutting edge of the defense industry, defending western Europe and Japan, their engineers and scientists are building Sony stereos and BMWs which are gobbling up significant chunks of our domestic market. It's a very significant issue, whether you can be at the cutting edge of both the economy and the military."[8]

R&D Measure 6: Share of Military R&D

The 1985 report of *Science Indicators* underscores the structural change toward military R&D and away from civilian R&D. In 1979, military R&D accounted for 49 percent of total R&D; in 1987 it is expected to rise to 73 percent. Including the weapons-related work of the Department of Energy, the total outlay in 1987 is slated to be $44.4 billion, while civilian R&D will remain at $16.4 billion (fig. 2.3).

Basic Research

Basic research (NMOR) of a generation or more ago paves the way for today's invention. Yet, because it remains out of sight, basic research is often out of mind, and the earliest victim of budget cuts.

Fig. 2.3
Military R&D as a Proportion of All Federal R&D

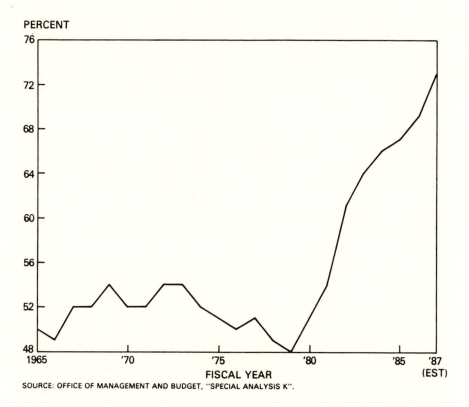

SOURCE: OFFICE OF MANAGEMENT AND BUDGET, "SPECIAL ANALYSIS K".

In spite of the 25 percent rise in 1987 to $44.4 billion, the military R&D is heavily weighted toward applied R&D:

The $44.4 billion proposed for military R&D in the departments of Defense and Energy is heavily weighted toward applied research and development. Less than 3 percent is officially designated as basic research.

Indeed, *DOD's [Department of Defense's] basic research would be held approximately constant between FY 1986 and FY 1987, at about the $1 billion level,* following a healthy increase from FY 1985 to FY 1986. Within this total, a new Universities Research Initiative would be continued . . . to support university facilities, high-risk academic research, fellowships, and multidisciplinary research centers . . . with a budget for FY 1986 of about $90 million . . . DOD officials are hoping to go up to about $100 million in FY. 1988, the third year of the program. [emphasis added][9]

Table 2.11a
Federal Obligations for Basic Research: Intramural and Federally Funded Research and Development Centers (FFRDC's) during fiscal year 1986.

Agency	Total (thousands of dollars)	Intramural (6)		FFRDC total (thousands of dollars)	Intramural and FFRDC (percentage)
		Total (thousands of dollars)	Percentage		
All agencies	7,875,126	1,969,165	25	852,433	36
Departments					
Agriculture	418,510	285,859	68	120	68
Commerce	17,521	16,113	92	112	93
Defense	964,446	342,750	36	13,390	37
Education	11,409	1,823	16	0	16
Energy	937,849	17,704	2	670,343	73
Health and Human Services	3,055,583	594,391	19	23,327	20
Interior	117,734	112,033	95	0	95
Justice	2,520	25	1	0	1
Labor	4,701	1,171	25	0	25
Transportation	3,300	300	9	0	9
Treasury	5,460	4,197	77	0	77
Other agencies					
Agency for International Development	2,941	78	3	0	3
Environmental Protection Agency	40,187	6,887	17	250	18
Federal Trade Commission	1,511	1,511	100	0	100
Library of Congress	288	288	100	0	100
National Aeronautics and Space Administration	835,000	347,703	42	34,644	46
National Science Foundation	1,364,865	145,031	11	110,247	19
Smithsonian Institution	71,001	71,001	100	0	100
Tennessee Valley Authority	4,700	4,700	100	0	100
Veterans Administration	15,600	15,600	100	0	100

Source: National Science Foundation

Table 2.11 presents the conduct of basic research by major departments and agencies.

Reallocation of Applied R&D to Basic Research

Frank Press, president of the National Academy of Sciences and chairman of the National Research Council, suggests that the budgetary crisis will probably endure for years, perhaps to the end of the century. The future growth in funds for basic research is likely to be almost flat, and in some cases, even negative.

He endorses the proposal by Erich Bloch, director of the National Science Foundation, to reallocate funds from applied R&D to basic research:

Table 2.11b
Examples of Basic Research Projects Conducted within Federal Agencies and FFRDCs.

Department or agency	Research area
Department of Energy	Atomic physics Heavy element chemistry Polymer science Radiation biology Climatology
Department of Defense	X-ray crystallography Geophysics Computer science Physical oceanography Astronomy and astrophysics Laser chemistry Operations research Mathematics Tribology
Department of Commerce	Meteorology Computer science Thermodynamics Fluid mechanics
National Aeronautics and Space Administration	Solar-terrestrial physics Cosmology Comparative planetology Astrophysics
Environmental Protection Agency	Photochemistry Separation science Atmospheric modeling Reproductive biology
Department of the Interior	Geology Geophysics Metallurgy Aquatic biology Ecology

Source: Frank Press, "The Best and the Worst of Times," *Science*, Vol. 231, 21 Mar 86, 1352. Copyright 1986 by the AAAS.

I support that proposal [of Erich Bloch asking for a major shift of resources toward the nation's universities, who argued that the funding should come from from a reallocation from applied research and development accounts, without any overall increase in the federal budget]. Something like a *2 percent reduction* in those accounts *would make $1 billion available* for the purpose, and the result would be an overwhelming improvement in our overall rate of technical progress. However, I would like to suggest that we reform not only the distribution of federal research and development funding, but also widen its availability on a competitive basis . . . .I suggest that, as is already the case with academic research, *intramural and* Federally Funded Research and Development Centers *(FFRDCs) research* be opened to a common peer-reviewed, national competition . . . from the universities, from national laboratories, and from agency laboratories. [emphasis added][10]

Press's argument is that one-quarter of federal support for basic research in FY86 is intramural funding. The share increases to one-third if FFRDC research is included, as shown in table 2.8.

If the Press proposal is adopted, it would make $2.85 billion available on a competitive basis. If the Bloch proposal is adopted, it would make $1 billion additionally available for basic research.

INSTRUCTION

To sustain inventions, sustained investment in instruction is indispensable. The foundation, of course, is trained talent.

Eroding Science and Technology Base of High School Education

Scientists and engineers, of course, constitute the substratum of research activity. It is precisely here that supply is falling behind demand. The 1985 *Science Indicators* presents for the first time a chapter on precollege science and mathematics education:

The average student in the age groups of 13 and 17 years *knows comparatively less about science and technology* than similar students did in earlier periods . . . .It is also worth noting that American high school students *take substantially less course work in science and math* than their counterparts in other major industrialized countries, and as a matter of fact, fewer courses than their parents about three decades ago. [emphasis added][11]

Eroding Base of Engineering Ph.Ds

Not only at entry levels, but also at existing levels, the trend is disturbing. Bloch argues (see fig. 2.4) that a smaller fraction of our best students are attracted to the sciences, and that the size of the relevant age groups is declining. He says further:

Equally disturbing is the decline in the number of engineering Ph.D.s since the early 1970s and the increasing proportion of degrees awarded to those who are not U.S. citizens. Since 1981, *more than half of all Ph.D. degrees in engineering in the United States have been awarded to foreign students. This proportion has risen in recent years*. The figures for mathematics and physics—the core disciplines of a technological society—are not much different.

Between 1980 and 1983, full-time graduate enrollment in science and engineering rose 6 percent overall. But enrollments of U.S. citizens rose only 1 percent, while *foreign student enrollment rose 23 percent*. Foreign students *accounted for 85 percent of the total growth* in this period. [emphasis added][12]

To help meet this serious problem, Bloch suggests using the NSF's successful model of engineering research centers to develop parallel basic science and

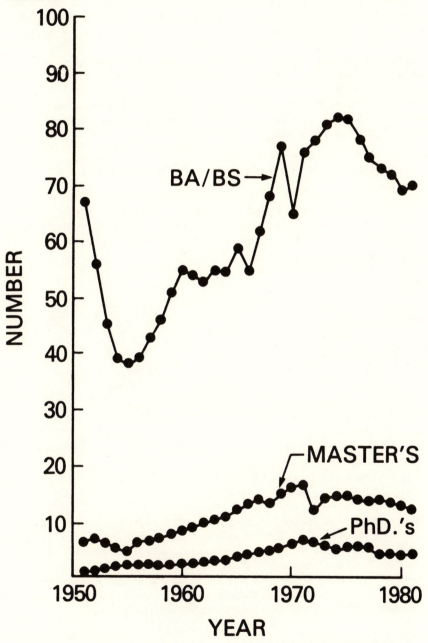

Fig. 2.4
Science/Engineering Degrees per Thousand Students in Appropriate Age Cohort, 1950–1981

Source: Erich Bloch, "Basic Research and Economic Health: The Coming Economic Challenge," *Science* Vol 232, 2 May 86, p. 596. Copyright 1986 by the AAAS.

technology centers. The engineering research centers have been successful because each focuses on an important area of engineering, and each brings together researchers from different disciplines and from both academia and industry:

> Like the Engineering Research Centers, Basic Science and Technology Centers should be multidisciplinary. It is at the intersection between the disciplines that one finds the most exciting work . . . .
>
> In our Engineering Research Centers and in other similar new programs we have insisted on substantial support from industry, and this should also be a requirement in Basic Science and Technology Centers.[13]

Expanding Base of Foreign-born Ph.Ds in Engineering and Science

While the fraction of U.S. students doing Ph.D work in engineering steadily decreases, the fraction of the foreign-born steadily increases. According to NSF figures, in the two decades from 1963–1983, the percentage of foreign-born doctoral students grew as follows:

Field	1963	1983
Industrial Engineering	7%	68%
Mechanical Engineering	28	60
Electrical Engineering	23	55
Chemical Engineering	22	52
Civil Engineering	37	63
Computer Science		40 (1986)

The enormous investment in educating the foreign-born at the doctoral level is borne by U.S. sources. As much as 57 percent of the five thousand foreign-born who won doctoral degrees in the sciences in 1986 told NSF that they intended to stay in the United States.

Herbert Simon thinks that U.S. investment in foreign-born doctoral students is paid back by those staying in the United States:

> They are paying for their long years of study with the most precious and expensive commodity, the one the *United States most needs today*: more knowledge, new knowledge, provided by their labor. By working in *American laboratories for three to seven years of post-graduate study*, thousands of young experts are by themselves the most efficient "subsidy" to scientific progress and economic developments. And a large majority of them do not choose, at graduation, the well-paid jobs offered by industry but remain in the tough, competitive life of *research and teaching*. [emphasis added][14]

R&D Measure 7: N/F Ratio

The problem is not that too many foreign-born apply to graduate programs, but that too few Americans do. The roots go back to the declining emphasis on science and mathematics in grade school curriculum, which is part of what we defined as "instruction."

The aptitude for the mathematical and the quantitative is indispensable to the flow of basic research talent in the future. The extremely wide variations in school systems throughout the United States requires that the innate abilities of students be measured consistently across the panorama of school environments. The Scholastic Aptitude Test (SAT) administered by the Educational Testing Service, Princeton, is now accepted most widely as a basis for undergraduate admissions. The aptitude portion of the Graduate Record Examination (GRE) is similarly required for graduate admissions.

To assess U.S. commitment to instruction, we could start with the SAT and GRE scores in specific categories. An aptitude index using SAT and GRE could easily show the ratio of the native-born/foreign-born applicants to graduate studies by field and score. The values of this N/F ratio can help calibrate the nation's progress toward improving the nurture of the plant of instruction.

MISSION VERSUS MARKET SURVIVAL

The four point zero million scientists and engineers in the country are subject to conflicting demands: DOD bidding for mission survival, industry bidding for market survival.

When industry commits resources to R&D, should it be for short-term returns from applied R&D; or should it be for long-term returns from basic research?

The conflict is continuous; therefore, we need to recognize its continuing presence in crucial R&D decisions. One viable framework is that of concomitant coalitions, which we will develop in the next chapter.

CONCLUDING OBSERVATIONS

We have developed the empirical referents of the total R&D resources available for both the country and corporations.

The dollar value of total R&D rose from $20.0 billion in 1965 to $118.6 billion in 1986. From a high of 2.9 percent of GNP in 1965, it fell to 2.2 in 1978, and then has risen steadily to 2.9 in 1986.

Of the three components of R&D, development is nearest to industry's heart, because it is development which brings the fruits of basic research and applied research closest to the marketplace. If basic research generates invention, applied research and development generate innovation.

If innovation is the fruit, invention is the flower, both of which are produced by instruction. Applying the principle "out of sight, out of mind," the least visible of the three—instruction—gets the short shrift under the first signs of a budget crunch, followed by the second least visible component, basic research.

How important is basic research to innovation? NSF study of ten innovations of "high social impact" ranging from the heart pacemaker to the video tape recorder in terms of "decisive events," shows that basic research dominated the preconception period, and that half of the basic research occurred 30 years before the first realization of the innovation. In other words, basic research fund cutting would be penny-wise and pound-foolish because its effects would be felt a whole generation later.

We developed a new ratio to measure the relationship between inn*O*vation and in*V*ention, the O/V ratio. Other measures are: monetary measure of basic research; numerical measure of potential inventors; potential inventors by industry; and degree by discipline of potential inventors and innovators.

Defense dominates research, since the beginning of the Cold War absorbing between one-third and one-half of the nation's scientific talent, now numbering four million scientists and engineers. The research done for mission does *not* generally translate into application to markets. R&D Measure 6 is the share of military R&D.

Foreign-born doctoral candidates take up engineering, avoided by the native-born. R&D Measure 7 is the ratio of native-born/foreign-born in GRE applications.

The conflict between basic research and applied R&D is continuous, as is that between missions and markets. A viable framework to handle this conflict, concomitant coalitions, is developed next.

3

Invention versus Improvement— Concomitant Coalitions (CONCOLs)

OVERVIEW: Faced with the choice between improvement of a present product(s) and the invention of a potential product(s), leading U.S. manufacturers have chosen the former. That choice has not only cost the market leader his leadership, but often his business as well.

A McKinsey study has shown that Du Pont, B. F. Goodrich, National Cash Register, and RCA, among others, have lost major markets because they gave top priority to defensive R&D at the expense of offensive R&D. By the same token, while RCA elected to stay with vacuum tubes and lost its leadership and market, Texas Instruments (TI) gambled its future on yet-to-be-invented semiconductors.

What RCA and TI demonstrate is the deliberate choice between present products and potential products, between short-term, almost-sure returns and long-term, uncertain returns. How should resources be allocated between conflicting objectives?

Coalitions are associations of opposing interests. Neumann-Morgenstern's theory of games develops discrete coalitions, such as those between A and B against C, or between A and C against B, or between B and C against A. In real life, however, it may be necessary to allow for A playing with and against B in the same game. The association of one party with and against the same party(ies) in the same game is called concomitant coalitions (CONCOLs).

CONCOLs require an inherent opposition of interests, which can be within the same entity (e.g., a corporation choosing between improvement and innovation). We could associate innovation with the alter-ego of the corporation (say, CEO) and improvement with the anti-ego (say, vice president for production). It should be noted that both executives are advocating the best for the corporation in their respective roles.

To give concreteness to the many opposing interests simultaneously working on technology management, we need to develop measures of CONCOL outcome in technology and territory. To move from the initial values of the outcome to the desired values, a CONCOL process is employed.

The five technology outcome measures are: (1) P/C, (2) R/R, (3) I/I, (4) RM/IR, and (5) N/M ratios. The four territory outcome measures are: (1) RM/IR, (2) F/F, (3) E/D, and (4) LT/ET ratios.

Empirical values for these ratios are illustrated. The deliberate determination of desired values for these ratios, and the deliberate policies to move the initial values to the desired values, contribute significantly to the corporation reaching out to its full potentials.

PRESENT PRODUCT VERSUS POTENTIAL PRODUCT

A bird in hand is not always worth two in the bush, at least when it comes to the hi-tech frontier. The former is the *improvement* of a present product(s), while the latter is the *invention* of a potential product(s).

Epitaphs of American Enterprises

We will discuss three instances of dramatic failure. In each case, the leading market shareholder of products embodying existing technology was replaced by minor unknowns which concentrated on innovative technology.

RCA was the leading manufacturer of vacuum tubes in 1955. In 25 years, RCA was out of the vacuum tube business; it was also out of the semiconductor business. In fact, none of the ten leading electronics manufacturers of the mid-1950s made the successful transition to the new technology of solid-state electronics.

Du Pont enjoyed a significant market share of nylon tire cords in the 1960s. Celanese worked on a product with inherently superior qualities—polyester. Ultimately Du Pont lost the market to polyester cords.

B. F. Goodrich was the leader in bias-ply tires in 1976. However, in three years, bias-ply tires were no longer supplied as original equipment; Michelin displaced bias-ply with radial tires.

These market leaders bet on the *improvement* of present products instead of the *invention* of potential products. Smaller companies which did bet on innovation won the market with their invention(s) of new technology, displacing those who bet on the improvement of their leading product(s) embodying existing technology.

Fighting the Future Instead of Flowing with It

Richard N. Foster, director of McKinsey & Co., says that the failure of RCA, Du Pont, and Goodrich is due to their fighting the future instead of flowing with it. He warns that similar attitudes can spell disaster for enterprises as disparate as computers and antiques, communications and antique dealerships:

Companies such as Du Pont, B. F. Goodrich, National Cash Register, and RCA, among many others, have all lost major markets and millions of dollars because of their *failure to manage technology . . .*

Defensive R&D is the top priority in many large corporations. It too is a wise thing to do UNLESS it *replaces offensive R&D*—and in many cases today it does. . . .

These troubles have plagued management in the past and are certainly going to be present in the future. *Computers, telecommunications, electronics,* most manufacturing operations, chemicals, drugs, *agricultural materials suppliers,* and service companies, banks and insurance companies, arbitrators, lawyers, consultants, even *antique dealers* are going to be vulnerable to technological change in the next 15 years. [emphasis added][1]

As each company in the forefront of the technology of the day pushes back known frontiers, how assuredly can it know that discontinuities, and not continuities, are what it should be pursuing?

On the successful side, recall how Texas Instruments' Patrick Haggerty postulated the search for discontinuity as policy: "During 1949 and 1950 it finally became clear to me that the future of electronics would be profoundly influenced by knowledge already attained and additional knowledge being rapidly gained about materials at the structure-of-matter level."[2]

Haggerty's strategy of finding the discontinuities was quite risky. He was committing 100 percent of the next four years' net profits. Given the prospects of keeping current profits as opposed to losing them, the latter choice obviously calls for decisively compelling reasons to assume such serious risk. The underlying conflict is one of perspectives: the short-term versus the long-term; the continuities versus the discontinuities.

CONFLICT AND COALITIONS

We may define conflict as the option to commit competing inputs for identical outputs (outcomes).

Coalitions

A coalition is the association of opposing interests. The interests are represented by individual(s), called party(ies). Coalitions are entered into by subsets of parties, such as individuals. If the same party (e.g., corporation) is involved in opposing interests (e.g., between short-term gains and long-term losses) the coalition members are subsets of the same player, the alter ego opting for long-term gains and the anti-ego opting for short-term gains.

Inherent Conflicts in R&D

We see a basic conflict between pursuing continuities and discontinuities. Continuities improve the performance characteristics of *present* products; discontinuities initiate and improve the performance characteristics of *potential* products. Improving present, proven products brings returns in the short run. However, investing in the future in uncertain products could bring returns in the long run.

The conflict is thus between present products and potential products, certain profits and uncertain profits, short-term returns and long-term returns, and continuities and discontinuities of performance characteristics.

This conflict is not resolved once and for all; it is a recurring issue which management has to face and resolve. The resolution does not necessarily mean the choice of one to the exclusion of the other.

It is critical to recognize the inherent opposition of interests, in this instance, between the short term and the long term. The corporation can choose to align itself "with" the short-term interests of quick returns, thereby aligning itself "against" the long-term interests of sustained returns. The decision facing the corporation is: *How should resources be allocated between conflicting objectives?*

Discrete Coalitions

In *Theory of Games and Economic Behavior*,[3] John von Neumann and Oskar Morgenstern discuss three-person games in which player A can join "with" player B, ipso facto aligning themselves "against" player C, to pursue maximization of returns to the coalition of A and B at the expense of C.

In the three-person game, which coalition—AB, BC, or AC— will be formed? It depends on two things: (1) the probability of more than 0.5 that the coalition outcome will be greater than the sum of the coalition member outcomes; and (2) the prior agreement on the distribution of the coalition outcome among coalition members (imputation).

Equally, if not more, important than the coalitions themselves is the bargaining that precedes their formation or non formation and/or dissolution. Bargaining is the process of offer and counteroffer of future outcome(s) in return for present association(s).

The three players A,B, and C are in conflict with each other. A is against B in that both A and B are trying to maximize their individual outcomes. When the total outcome is fixed, A's gain can be only at B's expense and vice versa.

In the Neumann-Morgenstern formulation, the coalitions are exclusive and exhaustive: A with B against C; A with C against B; and B with C against A.

CONCOMITANT COALITIONS

In real life, coalitions may not necessarily be as exclusive and exhaustive as the Neumann-Morgenstern coalitions, as illustrated by the following two real-life instances.

Concomitant Coalitions in Nuclear Survival

Consider the nuclear survival "game" or activity. The United States and France are both members of the North Atlantic Treaty Organization (NATO), and the Soviet Union is not. We present the opposing interests as:

United States with France against the Soviet Union on NATO

The first significant treaty to lessen the possibility of nuclear war was the Test Ban Treaty, which was signed by the United States, the Soviet Union, and most other nations, but not by France. The "game" or activity is still the same, namely, nuclear survival, in which the alignment of opposing interests are:

United States against France with the Soviet Union on Test Ban

Both NATO and the test ban are intergral elements of the same "game" of nuclear survival. We find that the same nations play "with" and "against" the same nations in the same game. They simultaneously compete and collaborate, forming opposing coalitions. This new concept in game theory was first defined in 1961:

Concomitant Coalitions (CONCOLs) are distinguished by the following features: (1) Simultaneous entry into coalition by players, (2) who band together for and against the same party at the same time, and (3) make moves subject to the several objectives of the different coalitions, but (4) governed ultimately by the over-riding principle of self-interest, (5) in order to achieve joint-profit-maximization, 6) in a non-zero-sum game.[4]

A concomitant coalition (CONCOL) is the association of one party with and against the same party(ies) in the same game (activity). The opposition can be within the same person, which we can characterize as the opposition of the alter ego and the anti-ego.

Time Horizon in R&D CONCOLs

The inherent opposition of interests can be within the same country or individual. In fact, the corporate choice between discontinuities and continuities in technology can be understood as the opposing advocacy by the alter ego and the anti-ego.

To the extent that the inherent conflict is time-related (e.g., short-term vs. long-term), the time horizon enters explicitly into policy considerations. In the case of RCA, the decision to stick with continued improvements—continuities— in the present successful technology of vacuum tubes represented the short-term perspective. That policy paid off in the short run in providing growth. The short-term growth in one technology, vacuum tubes, however, spelled death in its successor technology, semiconductors; the pursuit of short-term growth prevented long-term survival.

Associating the long-term survival with RCA's alter ego, we can represent the conflict as follows:

RCA alter ego with RCA long-term survival against short-term growth

RCA anti-ego against RCA long-term survival with short-term growth

But the alter ego advocacy of pursuing discontinuities could not guarantee that RCA would indeed discover any semiconductor technology, let alone the particular brand of technology which would capture market leadership. Therefore, the pursuit of discontinuities should be shown as being uncertain in outcome:

RCA alter ego with discontinuities pursuit with uncertain outcome with long-term survival against short-term growth

RCA anti-ego against discontinuities pursuit against uncertain outcome against long-term survival with short-term growth

The alter ego position is not against growth as much as it is for survival. If a choice has to be forced, the alter ego says, "Choose survival." The payoff in choosing survival is in the long term. If RCA had chosen to pursue semiconductors, it would probably have succeeded in capturing a significant market share, which would have continued to yield profits over the long term. It was these continued profits that the alter ego was urging RCA to bet on:

RCA alter ego with discontinuities pursuit with uncertain outcome with probable longer profit stream with long-term survival against short-term growth

RCA anti-ego against discontinuities pursuit against uncertain outcome against probable longer profit stream against long-term survival with short-term growth

The "longer-term profit stream" is not guaranteed. Quite conceivably, the potential product will require a period of initial losses before the break-even point.

An RCA official announced in 1958 that the corporation expected to lose $130 million in color televisions to reach the break-even point. How much does the $130 million represent in today's dollars? The consumer price index (CPI) stood at 100 in 1967 but rose to 320 in 1986.[5] It rose 81.5 percent between 1967 and 1977. Applying that rate retroactively to the preceding decade, we can estimate a CPI of 55 for 1958. The RCA decision to stand $130 million in losses until the new technology of color television took hold of the market represents $756 million in 1986 dollars. Three-quarters of a billion dollars is not an insignificant write-off.

Even with that substantial a commitment, RCA has not become the market leader in color television. In fact, foreign imports have flooded the consumer electronics market, including color television; and in May 1983 RCA, General Electric, and Zenith petitioned the U.S. International Trade Commission (ITC) that certain foreign imports of color television sets were injurious to U.S. industry. On April 6, 1984, the ITC issued a final ruling that the U.S. color television industry has been injured by imports from Korea and Taiwan.

Thus, even a significant underwriting of losses to launch a new technology can offer no assurance of achieving dominance of the market, let alone retaining it. But, if the corporation does not deliberately pursue discontinuities, it will have little chance of long-term survival and longer-term profit streams.

Real-life Roles of Alter Ego and Anti-Ego

The roles of the alter ego and the anti-ego are quite realistic in the U.S. corporation. The chief executive officer (CEO) is supposed to be so fully preoccupied with the long term that he would hardly know what goes on in the short term. On the other hand, the vice president of production would be so immersed in the short term that he would hardly be oriented to the long term. To designate their respective functional roles as alter ego and anti-ego is not to imply that either is less committed to the welfare of the corporation but simply that each is expected to advocate vigorously his assigned role and perspective.

It is not as though the alter ego or the anti-ego has to dominate. As a matter of fact, sometimes alter ego considerations overrule anti-ego considerations, and vice versa.

Defensive Versus Offensive R&D

Foster points out that defensive R&D is "a wise thing to do *unless* it replaces offensive R&D."[6] We can translate defensive R&D as *improvement*, and offensive R&D as *innovation*.

> Alter ego with innovation against improvement
>
> Anti-ego against innovation with improvement

How many resources should be allocated to defensive R&D, and how many to offensive R&D? Foster appears to suggest that both types of R&D should be pursued. What the CONCOL framework reveals is the inherent conflict between the two types of R&D competing for the same resources.

CONCOL OUTCOME MEASURES

Competitive cooperation between (among) opposing interests requires the specification of desirable outcomes as a target toward which the parties can progress. In chapter 2 we identified seven R&D measures which calibrate the outcome in country and corporate competition for the scarce resources of talent and treasure. We will now develop technology, territory (market), and time measures.

TECHNOLOGY OUTCOME MEASURES

The O/V ratio specifies the relative weight given to invention and innovation. Since the latter is the prime focus of industry, we will develop a measure that reflects industry commitment.

Technology Outcome 1: P/C Ratio

The numerator of the O/V ratio is innovation (applied R&D). Industry is vitally interested in innovation. It contributes (C) funds to development, and it performs (P) development. The P/C ratio dropped in 1986 to 61 percent of its 1965 value as seen from the following table; the industry's contribution of funds for development is rising. A desirable value for P/C can be targeted as an eventual outcome.

```
-------------------------------------------------------------
Year                 INDUSTRY SHARE IN
                Development           Development        (Performance)
                Performance           Funds             -------------
                (Performance)         (Contribution)    (Contribution
-------------------------------------------------------------

1965              77.0%                 33.7%               2.28

1975              78.1%                 51.0%               1.53

1986              76.6%                 54.2%               1.41

-------------------------------------------------------------
```

Basic Source: National Science Foundation

Technology Outcome 2: R/R Ratio

Corresponding to the input of faculty and facilities for basic research, what is the output of inventions? Edwin Mansfield studied 220 projects at three laboratories to determine four probabilities: (1) technical completion (of initiated projects); (2) commercialization (given completion); (3) market success (given commercialization); and (4) market success (given project initiation).[7]

He found the probability of technical completion to be 0.68 at Lab X, 0.66 at Lab Y, and 0.52 at Lab Z. If the three labs were equal in size, the probability for all laboratories would be 0.62. Allowing for their unequal size, Mansfield found the probability for all laboratories to be 0.57.

Of course, there are wide variations in the type of research projects. For instance, the probability of success of the project to invent (e.g., semiconductors) is likely to be less than the probability of success of the project to improve (e.g., the performance of vacuum tubes). The theoretical value of the probability runs from 0 to 1.

We can choose as the initial value of the CONCOL outcome either the probability of technical completion for all laboratories, 0.57, or for a particular laboratory X, 0.68.

Technology Outcome 3: I/I Ratio

Let us consider the probability of technical completion as the probability of invention; and the probability of commercialization as the probability of innovation. The Mansfield results are as follows:

Laboratory	Probability of Technical Completion	Prob. of Commercialization Given Technical Completion
Laboratory X	0.68	0.71
Laboratory Y	0.66	0.59
Laboratory Z	0.52	0.49
ALL LABORATORIES	0.57	0.55

Source: Mansfield et al. data

Technology Outcome 4: RM/IR Ratio

The relationship between input and output in research projects is at best a nominal measure of the underlying substantive characteristics. We will consider two substantive characteristics: (1) limits of the rate of advances in technology; and (2) linear extensions and quantum jumps in behavioral properties.

The first characteristic tells us that the rate of increase in the technological characteristics will decrease. In chapter 8, we will consider Richard Foster's study of Du Pont's incremental investment to improve the performance of tire cord. But we will use the insight of his analysis here. He found that the first $60-million R&D investment yielded 800 percent improvement in tire-cord performance. We calculated the percent improvement to be 13.3 per million dollars, but we see that the next $15 million brings only 1.7 per million, and the next $25 million, only 0.2 per million.

What is more important than the actual values of performance improvement/ R&D investment is the point of inflection—where the curve changes direction.

Improvements in the product performance (e.g., nylon cord) keep coming at a rapid rate (e.g., 13.3 percent); then it slows down (e.g., 1.7 percent); and then it begins to decline (e.g., 0.2 percent).

What is particularly significant is the change from rapid growth to maturity (RM), which signals that the well of invention is beginning to dry up. We can calibrate it in terms of the change from infancy to rapid growth in the improvements in the performance characteristics. The CONCOL outcome measure is the RM/IR ratio.

Technology Outcome 5: N/M Ratio

The second substantive measure of technology characterizes the two different types of technological change. In the first substantive measure, the change in technology was movement along the same curve. In addition, we need to consider technology which jumps across curves.

Linear Extension of Performance Characteristics

Consider the safe storage of milk. Boiling is one method which extends the safe period of storage from minutes to hours. The extension of the period from minutes to hours is the linear extension of performance characteristics. Linear extension soon reaches a limit. By boiling the milk for hours instead of minutes, its safe storage period cannot be extended beyond several hours.

Quantum Jump in Performance Characteristics

Refrigeration provides a quantum jump in the safe period of storage—from minutes and hours to days.

Temperature is the dimension in which the quantum jump in the performance characteristics has taken place—from a few hours to days, and even weeks.

Size is another dimension in which the quantum jump in technology brought about the transformation of industry from aircraft to missiles.

"Structure-of-matter level" knowledge which changed the course of not only Texas Instruments, but also of the semiconductor industry in the United States itself, was a forecast of discontinuities. The existing technology was that of vacuum tubes. No conceivable pattern of the growth of vacuum tube performance characteristics could suggest the dramatic jump into semiconductor technology.

Quantum Jumps, Not Mere Linear Extensions

Improvements in existing technology are linear extensions of performance characteristics, while inventions represent discontinuities—quantum jumps. We represent these quantum jumps in figure 3.1.

N/M Ratio

Linear extensions can be considered from the point of view of change in performance characteristics ("more of the same") while quantum jumps can be considered "none of the same" (N/M ratio).

Fig. 3.1
Quantum Jumps in Performance Characteristics

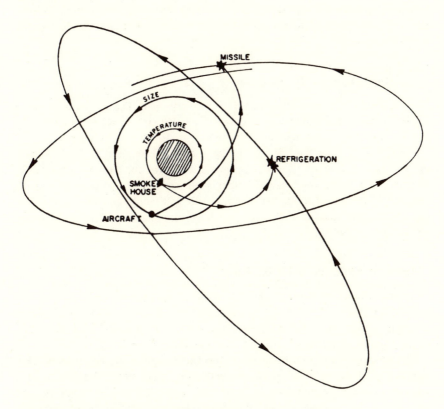

TERRITORY OUTCOME MEASURES FOR CONCOL

The RM/IR ratio applies to the territory (market) as well.

Territory Outcome 1: RM/IR Ratio

The rate of market penetration starts slowly (infancy), gathers momentum (rapid growth), and later runs out of steam (maturity). As the maturity point is reached, the returns to increasing advertising and promotion efforts will decrease. If the corporation keeps watch over its rate of penetration per unit of effort, the IR changes and RM changes can be spotted, permitting timely actions to be taken.

Territory Outcome 2: F/F Ratio

Maturity is recognized best after the fact—when it is too late to take action. Therefore, we need an earlier indicator.

Select a smaller value than 100 percent as a corporation's targeted market share, say 30 percent. Given a specific target, divide it by 2: 15 percent. How long does it take to acquire half of the target market share? If it takes X units to acquire the first half of the market, how long does it take to acquire the final half—2X? The ratio of the time, final half/first half, or F/F ratio can be a useful CONCOL outcome.

Territory Outcome 3: E/D Ratio

Increasingly, the territory (market) is international. The corporation could select a specific target share of the domestic market (D), as we saw earlier, and in addition, select a specific share of the export (E), or foreign market.

Instead of targeting the F/F ratio in domestic and foreign markets separately, the interrelationship between the two markets may be recognized in the the E/D ratio. How many units should be exported per unit of domestic sale of the product? If the domestic market is pursued first, it would be some time before exports emerge, making E/D zero, which we designate as 0.01, to avoid the difficulties of division by zero.

Territory Outcome 4: LT/ET Ratio

Export of products is important; but export of technology can be critical. We said earlier that the United States is generally ahead in invention, while Japan is ahead in innovation. How can the asset of U.S. invention be used profitably, to the mutual advantage of exporter and importer?

The new invention that gives the competitive edge to the corporation itself will be supplanted by newer inventions in the same technology. If the technology level of the new invention is 100, that of the newer technology would be say, 115. Let us also say that the 115 technology was invented 12 months after the 100.

Other corporations in the United States and other countries would welcome the opportunity to license the 100-level technology when the corporation has already moved on to innovations embodying the 115-level invention. However, the corporation may cut its own throat by licensing so close a level of technology to a competitor who did not have to spend the millions of dollars in risky R&D to develop the 100 technology. For one thing, the 100 is too close to the 115 for comfort, possibly permitting the licensee to make a close substitute at much lower cost.

However, consider a country at technology level 15. If it can license a higher level technology, say 45, from the corporation, that increases the country's technology level to 300 percent—with none of the risks of failure, none of the millions of dollars in R&D, none of the allocation of R&D personnel that were crucial to achieving the 45 level.

The licensing is mutually beneficial. The 45-level technology is 55 points below the technology embedded in the current product(s) of the corporation; therefore, it cannot threaten the corporation's market. Further, to ensure that the recipient country does adopt the transferred technology of level 45, the country should develop viable marketing plans for products imbedding the 45 technology abroad, and the corporation should receive a share of the new market on a sliding scale, thus encouraging the country to expand its market.

Let us say that the corporation further offers to license a higher level technology (e.g., level 60), to the country if it scrupulously observes the letter and spirit of the technology transfer.

The corporation receives income from two sources: (1) licensing fee for technology 45; and (2) share of the new foreign market that is developed by the recipient country for the product(s) imbedding 45. The country receives: (1) a rise in technology level to 300 percent in the very first round; (2) a rise in technology level to 400 percent in the second round; (3) the opportunity to create a new product(s) imbedding a technology level which is 300 percent of its current level; (4) the opportunity to create a new market abroad for the 45-level product(s); (5) the opportunity to create a new product(s) imbedding a technology level which is 400 percent of its current level; and (6) the opportunity to create a new market abroad for the 60-level product(s).

This mutually beneficial technology transfer between the corporation and the foreign country (or domestic corporation[s]) can be calibrated in terms of the successive levels of higher technology achieved in the technology transfer. The ratio of the later technology (60) over the earlier technology (45) would be the territory measure: LT/ET. The initial value will be 1; the higher the LT, the higher the ratio.

CONCLUDING OBSERVATIONS

We have developed a concept which provides a framework to allocate funds between country and corporate R&D, or between mission and market R&D.

We have found that the conflict is even more widespread; it can additionally be between present products and potential products, certain profits and uncertain profits, short-term returns and long-term returns, and continuities and discontinuities of performance characteristics.

Since the failure to recognize these continuing conflicts has caused epitaphs to be written of many a flourishing U.S. enterprise, a concept which provides a framework in which to recognize the inherent opposition of interests emerges as imperative.

We developed the concept of concomitant coalition (CONCOL)—the association of one party with and against the same party(ies) in the same game (activity).

The opposition can reside in the same person, corporation, or country. To give concreteness to the opposition, it is convenient to speak of "alter ego" and "anti-ego."

For instance, when RCA announced in 1958 that the corporation expected to lose $ 130 million in color television to reach the break-even point, it could be interpreted as the ''alter ego'' of RCA joining ''with'' the long term. Since there was no guarantee in 1958 that RCA would succeed, the ''alter ego'' was joining ''with'' the probable profit stream which could last longer than $ 130 million invested for short-term surer gains from products based on continuing technology.

RCA managers producing products which are currently profitable may well argue against throwing away $130 million on a product based on a new technology, because both the feasibility of the product and the generation of the market have to be proven sometime in the future. They could opt for short-term security against long-term potential. That position could be described as that of the ''anti-ego.''

To make the CONCOL concept operational, we developed CONCOL outcome measures for technology and territory. The five technology outcome measures are: (1) RM/IR, (2) P/C, (3) R/R, (4) I/I, and (5) N/M ratios. The four territory outcome measures are: (1) RM/IR, (2) F/F, (3) E/D, and (4) LT/ET ratios.

Two values are associated with each ratio: initial outcome and desired outcome. Empirical values of these outcome measures are developed, providing illustrative desired outcomes to be achieved.

The battle raging between the United States and Japan on hi-tech can result in mutual slaughter. CONCOLs offer the alternative of joint survival, as outlined in the next chapter.

4   *Chips to Ceramics: Mutual Slaughter or Joint Survival?*

OVERVIEW: The Japanese sweep of the world market for hi-tech products well before they are manufactured on a large scale contains the potential of U.S. retaliation because the mounting Japanese trade surplus is built on unfair tactics. If a $37-billion surplus in 1984 stirred a lethargic Senate to ask President Reagan to force open the Japanese markets, still higher surpluses and still inaccessible Japanese markets are bound to force matters to a head sooner than later.

To identify the areas of hi-tech that precipitate friction between the United States and Japan, we classify major technological changes into two types: linear extension of performance characteristics, such as the preserving of milk for a few hours by boiling it; and quantum jumps in performance characteristics, such as the preserving of milk for days instead of hours through refrigeration.

Linear extensions and quantum jumps are visualized in the 20 selected technology areas for military missions. The Defense Advanced Research Projects Agency's (DARPA) Strategic Computing Program seeks to realize operationally many human-like capabilities in machines by 1990. The application in each service focuses attention upon the application of artificial intelligence to military missions.

More quantum jumps than linear extensions are in the cards for electronics, materials, and biotechnology. In particular, one of the concentrations of Japan in the materials area is ceramics. The potential application of ceramics to integrated circuits makes this Japanese research significant to military missions as well, not to speak of the Japanese sweep of a good part of the $10-billion market by 1990.

The United States can deny Japan the territory for its technology—a negative-sum game in which both lose. Or the United States can exchange Japanese technology for U.S. territory for a period of time—a positive-sum game in which both gain.

MUTUAL SLAUGHTER IN TECHNOLOGY AND TERRITORY

The sweep of world markets by Japan in hi-tech areas, one after the other, and the invasion of the U.S. domestic market, have put progressive strains on U.S.-Japanese relations.

"The Situation Is Very Bad"

Japan's deputy foreign minister for economic affairs, Mr. Reishi Teshima, arriving in New York on April 4, 1985, en route to Washington to diffuse the escalating trade crisis between his country and the United States, said, "The situation is very bad."[1]

Two days earlier, the U.S. Senate Finance Committee passed a bill requiring President Reagan to take action against Japanese imports through higher tariffs or quotas if he was unable to persuade Japan to open its doors to more U.S. goods within 90 days. The Commerce Committee of the U.S. House of Representatives was considering a similar bill.[2]

Japan's $37-billion surplus in trade with the United States in 1984 precipitated legislative determination to do something about Japan's unfair trade policies. Said U.S. Senator Frank Lautenberg: "We don't want to start a trade war, but we must convince them to play fair."[3]

Spectre of Losing the Biggest Market

Although four years later, Japan's trade doors were hardly any more open to U.S. exports and the trade surplus had grown to $45 billion in favor of Japan, no drastic actions were taken. However, Japan could win many battles, and still lose the war. The United States is the world's most lucrative market; and if Congress is sufficiently roused, restrictive walls can be erected. The growing perception that Japan is unfair in trade with the United States can, in the extreme, result in massive retribution in the form of exclusion from entry altogether. While the chances are extremely slim for such a sweeping action, it should raise an unpleasant spectre.

Technology and Territory

Japan has been conquering world markets (territory) through impressive gains in hi-tech. She has actually been preselling advanced technology products which have yet to be manufactured on a large scale. To assess the issues in the Japanese-U.S. friction in territory, we must look at the technology. It is the change in technology that is at issue.

TECHNOLOGY FOR MISSIONS/MARKETS

While survival in world markets is of utmost urgency, the issue of U.S. survival in a war is of paramount importance. Further, the sweep of markets by Japan includes hi-tech areas, such as ceramics, which can make a critical difference in the military survival of the United States. Therefore, we will first discuss the survival technology areas for military missions, and then markets.

MISSION APPLICATION 5: U.S.-SOVIET SCORECARD OF SURVIVAL TECHNOLOGY AREAS OF MILITARY MISSIONS

We saw in chapter 3 that military R&D has dominated R&D in both funding and personnel, commanding about three out of four dollars, and one out of two scientists and engineers. Military R&D has spearheaded foundational developments in semiconductors, computers, integrated circuits, and the like. What areas of technology have been currently chosen by the military as critical for the future survival of the country?

Beginning in 1979, the secretary of defense and the under secretary of defense for research, development, and acquisition have presented to Congress major technology areas in which the United States and the Soviet Union are competing in weaponry. The unclassified report also gives the current standing of each country: United States superior; Soviet Union superior; United States/Soviet Union equal. More importantly, it shows the perceived tendencies at present: the United States is superior, but is losing the lead.

Basic Technology Areas

Table 4.1 lists 20 most important basic technology areas. According to the U.S. Department of Defense, in five areas, the United States and Soviet Union are equal. In eight areas, the United States is superior. In six areas, the United States is moving toward equality with the Soviet Union. In one area, computers and software, the United States is advancing its lead over the Soviet Union.

Technology in Deployed Military Systems—Strategic

Table 4.2 details relative U.S./Soviet technology level in deployed military systems.

In four of the eight strategic deployed systems, the United States is superior; in three, the Soviet Union is superior; and in one, the United States and Soviet Union are equal.

In two of the strategic deployed systems, U.S. superiority is slipping.

Table 4.1

Relative U.S./Soviet Standing in the Twenty Most Important Basic Technology Areas*

Basic Technologies	U.S. Superior	U.S./USSR Equal	USSR Superior
1. Aerodynamics/Fluid Dynamics		X	
2. Computers and Software	◄—X		
3. Conventional Warheads (Including all Chemical Explosives)		X	
4. Directed Energy (Laser)		X	
5. Electro-Optical Sensor (Including Infrared)	X		
6. Guidance and Navigation	X		
7. Life Sciences (Human Factors/Biotechnology)	X		
8. Materials (Lightweight, High Strength, High Temperature)	X —►		
9. Micro-Electronic Materials and Integrated Circuit Manufacturing	X		
10. Nuclear Warheads		X	
11. Optics		X	
12. Power Sources (Mobile) (Includes Energy Storage)		X	
13. Production/Manufacturing (Includes Automated Control)	X		
14. Propulsion (Aerospace and Ground Vehicles)	X —►		
15. Radar Sensor	X —►		
16. Robotics and Machine Intelligence	X		
17. Signal Processing	X		
18. Signature Reduction	X		
19. Submarine Detection	X —►		
20. Telecommunications (Includes Fiber Optics)	X		

* 1. The list is limited to 20 technologies, which were selected with the objective of providing a valid base for comparing overall U.S. and USSR basic technology. The list is in alphabetical order. These technologies are "on the shelf" and available for application. (The technologies are not intended to compare technology levels in currently deployed military systems.)

2. The technologies selected have the potential for significantly changing the military capability in the next 10 to 20 years. The technologies are not static; they are improving or have the potential for significant improvements; new technologies may appear on future lists.

3. The arrows denote that the relative technology level is changing significantly in the direction indicated.

4. Relative comparisons of technology levels shown depict overall average standing only; countries may be superior, equal or inferior in subcategories of a given technology.

5. These average assessments can incorporate a significant variance when the individual components of a technology are considered.

Source: Department of Defense, ''The FY 1987 DOD Programs for Research and Development,'' Statement by Undersecretary of Defense Research and Engineering to the 99th Congress, 1986, II–11.

Table 4.2
Relative U.S./Soviet Technology Level in Deployed Military Systems*

System Type	U.S. Superior	U.S./USSR Equal	USSR Superior
Strategic Warfare			
Intercontinental Ballistic Missiles		X	
Ballistic Missile Submarines	X		
Submarine Launched Ballistic Missiles	X →		
Bombers	X		
Surface-To-Air Missiles (SAMs)	No U.S. System Deployed		
Ballistic Missiles Defense	No U.S. System Deployed		
Anti-Satellite			← X
Cruise Missiles	X →		
Tactical Warfare			
Land Warfare			
SAMs (Including Naval)		X	
Tanks		X	
Artillery			X
Infantry Combat Vehicles		X	
Anti-Tank Guided Missiles		X	
Attack Helicopters	X		
Chemical Warfare			X
Tactical Ballistic Missiles		X	
Air Warfare			
Fighter/Attack and Interceptor Aircraft	X →		
Air-To-Air Missiles	X		
Air-To-Surface Munitions	X →		
Airlift Aircraft	X		
Naval Warfare			
Attack Submarines	X →		
Torpedoes	X →		
Sea Based Aircraft	X		
Surface Combatants	X →		
Naval Cruise Missile		X	
Mines			X
Other			
Command, Control, Communications and Intelligence			
Communications		X	
Electronic Countermeasures/ECCM		X	
Early Warning	X		
Surveillance & Reconnaisance	X		
Training Simulators	X		

*1. These are comparisons of system technology level only, and are not necessarily a measure of effectiveness. The comparisons are not dependent on scenario, tactics, quantity, training or other operational factors. Systems farther than 1 year from IOC are not considered.

2. The arrows denote that the relative technology level is changing significantly in the direction indicated.

3. Relative comparisons of technology levels shown depict overall average standing only; countries may be superior, equal or inferior in subcategories of a given technology in a deployed military system.

Source: Department of Defense, ''The FY 1987 DOD Programs for Research and Development,'' Statement by the Undersecretary of Defense Research and Engineering to the 99th Congress, 1986, II–12

Technology in Deployed Military Systems—Tactical

With respect to tactical deployed military systems, the United States is superior in nine, and the Soviet Union is superior in two. In seven both are equal. In five out of the nine, the Soviet Union is losing its superiority.

Technology in Command, Control, Communications, and Intelligence C^3I

The United States is superior in the three deployed C^3I systems, as well as in the technology of training simulators.

Criteria for U.S. Investment in Specific Technology Areas

Of the 20 technology areas, which one(s) should the United States concentrate on primarily? To choose one over another, the contribution to the national security objective by the former should be greater than that of the latter. What is the objective?

Deterrence Measure 1: Delivered Destruction Ratio (DDR)

Deterrence probably epitomizes the national security objective. To deter a would-be adversary, it must be convinced that the United States will inflict unacceptable damage upon it. Such a conviction is Soviet credibility in U.S. capability.

The unacceptability of damage comes from a ratio (theirs/ours) which is greater than 1. In other words, the damage that "they" can inflict upon us is greater than the damage that "we" can inflict upon them. We need an integrated measure which combines the megatonnage, the circular error of probability, the strategic doctrine, the will-to-use weapons, and the like.

We propose the delivered destruction ratio (DDR) as such a measure. By insisting on "delivered" destruction, we insist that we go beyond counting warheads or delivery platforms. Further, DDR should always be expressed as a ratio, ours/theirs being desired to be greater than 1 to indicate our superiority. Of course, the same sentiment will be reciprocated by our would-be adversary.

Deterrence Measure: Initial Values of DDR by Armed Service

Technology areas are pursued to imbed their advances in deployed systems. The deployed systems are armed services-specific—those of the Army, Air Force, or Navy. Therefore, the DDR should be calibrated with reference to each service. What is the initial value of DDR (ours/ theirs) for the U.S. Army, U.S. Navy, and U.S. Air Force?

If the DDR is equal, the ratio (ours/theirs) will be 1, or 100 percent, which we can multiply by 100. If we are less than equal, the DDR (ours/theirs) will be say, 93, instead of 100. Whatever the initial value what should be the eventual value?

Deterrence Measure 2: Attributed Share by Armed Service

The increase in the DDR value that each service would like to accomplish should be weighted by its share of the DOD budget. If each service were equally important to national security, each should get 33.3 percent of the DOD budget. Departures from that figure reflect the judgement on the part of Congress of the higher or lower contribution of each service. Since the entire DOD budget is to ensure deterrence, the service share of the DOD budget is the estimate of the service contribution to deterrence.

Deterrence Measure 3: Promising Technology Areas for Each Service

To move from the initial to the eventual DDR value, what technology area(s) would possibly bring about the most improvements in particular modernization efforts—strategic and/or tactical? If say, the two most important technology areas for the most promising weapons systems of each service were to be identified, the technology areas which are coveted by all the services will emerge.

Deterrence Measure 4: Areas of U.S. Superiority over the Soviet Union

Computers and software is likely to emerge as one of the most sought-after technology areas. Computers permeate the operations of virtually all weapon systems. Those who command the field are most likely to succeed be it in missions or in markets.

Each service attaches different degrees of importance to each of the leading technologies: Army—materials technology, 60 percent; computers and software technology, 40 percent.; Navy—materials, 75 percent; guidance, 25 percent.

Deterrence Measure 5: Areas of Declining Lead of the United States over the Soviet Union

While improving in the technology areas in which it is in the lead, the United States would also want to retain leadership in other areas where its lead is slipping. Such areas are also likely to appear in the choice by services of desired technology areas. The DOD can assign weights to the areas of U.S. superiority and areas of slipping superiority.

Resource Allocation to Technology Areas

We have developed five deterrence measures which together will help determine what share of R&D funds should be allocated to specific technology areas crucial to the military missions of the country.

Strategic Computing Program

The one basic technology area in which U.S. superiority is increasing is computers and software. The Defense Advanced Research Projects Agency (DARPA) has launched an ambitious program to make headway in several fronts in computers and software:

The overall goal of the program is to provide the United States with a broad base of machine intelligence technology that will greatly increase our *national security and economic power*. This technology promises to yield strong new *defense systems* for use against *massed forces*, and thus to raise the threshold and decrease the chances of major conflict. [emphasis added][4]

To develop a broad base of machine intelligence capability for defense, three military applications have been chosen, one in each service: (1) autonomous vehicles—Army; (2) battle management—Navy; and (3) pilot's associate—Air Force. Figure 4.1 presents the program structure and goals.

MARKET APPLICATION 3: U.S.-JAPANESE SCORECARD OF SURVIVAL TECHNOLOGY AREAS FOR MARKETS

DARPA's strategic computing aims primarily at national defense. Advances in machine intelligence application to national defense are most likely to have spillover effects in nondefense areas.

Japan's National Commitment Conspicuous by Its Absence in the United States

However, there is no unified response to the mighty challenge from Japan which has launched a most visible and conserted effort to launch by 1990 the prototype fifth-generation computer system. With no national effort, the U.S. Senate phrased its inquiry in terms, not of what technology areas the United States selected to succeed in domestic and foreign markets, but what Japan selected. The General Accounting Office (GAO) wrote to Senator Lloyd Bentsen, vice chairman of the Subcommittee on Economic Goals and Intergovernmental Policy of the Joint Economic Committee:

In your February 8, 1983, letter, you requested that we provide information on how much research and development (R&D) the U.S. government was conducting or funding in the 12 specific areas of *electronics, materials, and biotechnology* that had been selected for *support by the Japanese government....*

Six of the areas are related to *materials technology,* while three are part of electronics technology. The six areas in materials are: ceramics, composite materials, polymer separation membranes, conducting polymers, crystalline polymers, and controlled crystal

Fig. 4.1
Program Structure and Goals—DARPA

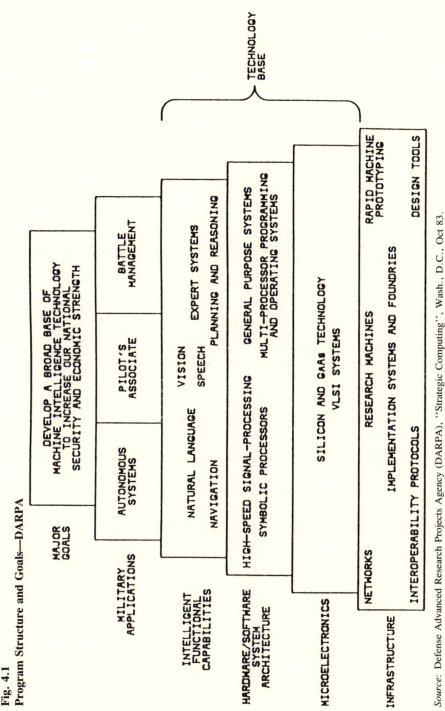

Source: Defense Advanced Research Projects Agency (DARPA), "Strategic Computing", Wash., D.C., Oct 83.

Table 4.3
Japanese Government Funding Levels for New Technology Programs*
($ Millions)

	FY 1981	FY 1982	FY 1983	TOTAL
New Materials	$6.2	$11.2**	$13.7	$31.1
New Electronic Devices	3.1	4.9	6.2	14.2
TOTAL	9.3	16.1	19.9	45.3

* Excludes biotechnology, which is not covered in this report
**Excludes other ceramic research outside of this program

Source: U.S. General Accounting Office

alloys. The *three electronics* areas are: super-lattice devices, three-dimensional circuit cells, and devices with high resistance to heat and nuclear radiation.

As agreed, we did not develop information on the three biotechnology areas in the original request because of ongoing work in the Office of Technology Assessment. [emphasis added][5]

Comparative Funding in Future Technology—Japan and the United States

Table 4.3 shows the $45-million funding for new materials and electronic devices during FY81–83 by Japan, and table 4.4 the $417-million funding by the United States, approximately ten times as much.

MARKET APPLICATION 4: JAPANESE "CERAMIC FEVER"

Two-thirds of Japan's funding for new technology during the three years FY81–83 was devoted to new materials.

$10-Billion Market

The Materials Research Society held its 1986 spring meeting in Palo Alto, California during April 15–19, 1986. The number of presentations more than doubled from 50 in 1984 to 117 in 1986. Ceramics, which encompass most inorganic materials except metals, were hailed as the up-and-coming marvel:

With a market heading toward *$10 billion* or more by the end of the decade, advanced ceramics are the hot commodity at the moment, and practitioners of the trade such as

Table 4.4
Distribution of Fiscal Year 1983 Funding for Specific Materials and Electronics R&D Areas Within Six U.S. Federal Agencies

	DOD	DOE	NASA	NSF	NBS	BOM	TOTAL
Composites	$84.0	$ 2.3	$13.9	$0.1	$ 0.3	$ -	$100.6
Ceramics	15.8	20.0	1.9	2.8	2.3	1.6	44.4
Rapid Solidification	18.7	3.1	2.4	2.6	1.0	1.4	29.2
Polymers-Crystal	3.3	5.0	0.2	2.0	1.0	-	11.5
Polymers-Synthetic	1.6	2.0	0.1	0.7	-	-	4.4
Polymers-Membranes	-	0.9	-	-	0.1	-	1.0
TOTAL	123.4	33.3	18.5	8.2	4.7	3.0	191.1

THREE ELECTRONIC DEVICES AREAS

	DOD	DOE	NASA	NSF	NBS	BOM	TOTAL
Fortified ICs	$ 6.9	$11.6	$ 0.4	$ -	$0.3	$ -	$19.2
Superlattice	8.8	1.0	0.3	0.3	-	-	10.4
3-D ICs	3.2	1.7	-	0.2	-	-	5.1
TOTAL	18.9	14.3	0.7	0.5	0.3	-	34.7
GRAND TOTAL	142.3	47.6	19.2	8.7	5.0	3.0	225.8

Source: U.S. General Accounting Office

David Clark of the University of Florida are saying that *ceramics* will be to the *1990s* what *polymers* were to the *1970s*. [emphasis added][6]

Present and Future Uses

Integrated circuits and automobiles are the prime areas of use:

Right now the single largest use for advanced ceramics is in electrically *insulating integrated circuit packages* and substrates. . . . However, the "glamour" ceramics are those being developed for high-temperature engines for *future automobiles*. [emphasis added][7]

Japan's Sweep of the Ceramics Market

As in the case of fifth-generation computer systems, Japan has concentrated its efforts on ceramics; it is struck by "ceramic fever."

One of the striking features of the fifth-generation computer systems is the cooperation among competing companies in the research and development of the future technology. As soon as the new technology becomes operational, the companies convert the invention into innovation, and compete in the marketplace.

In the United States, the antitrust laws discourage cooperation in R&D among competitive corporations for fear of violating antitrust regulations.

Another striking feature of Japanese enterprise is its "win the (world) market first" strategy. Ceramics is no exception:

Of particular concern is the rapid progress of Japanese research and development in these materials relative to that in the United States. . . . Integrated circuit packages provide one motivation for this concern. Michael Kelley of the Department of Commerce told those attending the conference last July 1985 at the National Bureau of Standards on the future of the U.S. advanced ceramics industry that *a single Japanese company*, Kyoto Ceramics (known as Kyocera in the United States), which also makes those "new stone age" ceramic scissors and knives that are now widely available, *has captured almost two-thirds of this market*.

The glamour ceramics for high-temperature engines give even more cause for concern. . . . The Japanese jumped in much later than 1971 when the US federal agencies worked on advanced ceramics but already *Nissan has begun selling*, so far only in Japan and in limited numbers, deluxe model cars equipped with *turbochargers having ceramic parts*, while *Isuzu* has been offering since 1981 a similarly limited number of vehicles with diesel engines having *ceramic glow plugs and precombustion chambers*. The fear is that *losing the race to the next generation ceramics automobile engine* would have immense economic consequences. [emphasis added][8]

SLAUGHTER OR SURVIVAL?

Japan is clearly ahead in its sweep of world markets and penetration of the U.S. domestic market in key hi-tech areas. Insofar as areas such as ceramics hold potentials for military missions, displacement of the United States in technology and territory may be viewed with sufficient alarm to resort to drastic measures.

A hi-tech inventor may enjoy the monopoly advantage of six months to two years, by which time others will catch up and even jump ahead. The inventor with technology and no territory will be unable to cash in on his invention. Therefore, Japan would not want to gain short-term inroads into the U.S. market at the peril of being banished altogether.

CONCOL requires a balancing of quid pro quos, such as technology for territory. Japan can enjoy access to the United States and other markets for a specified time period in return for licensing of Japanese technology to the United States. The time period will allow Japan to reap the benefits of being the first with the invention, while the United States enjoys access to the hi-tech invention.

The alternative to CONCOL is denial of territory to Japan and denial of technology to the United States, a negative-sum game in which both parties lose.

CONCLUDING OBSERVATIONS

We have developed the areas of hi-tech which affect mission and market survival of the United States.

The reactive nature of the U.S. approach to hi-tech is shown by the Congress asking the GAO to study 12 specific areas of electronics, materials, and biotechnology selected for support by the Japanese government.

Two-thirds of Japan's investment in new research is devoted to new materials. Ceramics leads the way. A projected $10-billion market by 1990 has generated "ceramics fever" in Japan. Its application to integrated circuits holds promise for military missions in addition to the civilian market.

Funding levels in Japan are modest by comparison with the United States in the areas of electronics, materials, and biotechnology. However, the Japanese national commitment to them is conspicuous by its absence in the United States.

One of the electronics areas is the fifth-generation computer system. The arrangement under which major electronics manufacturers cooperate to do research in selected areas, in order that they may compete in the marketplace by embodying the results of the joint research, provides an excellent working example of CONCOL.

To explore CONCOL's application to U.S.-Japanese relations, a quid of Japanese technology pro quo of American territory for a specified period may provide a useful starting point. A U.S.-Japanese CONCOL will primarily be concerned with the market.

Turning from markets to missions, we have examined in some detail 20 specific technology areas in most of which the United States leads the Soviet Union. In the several areas in which the U.S. lead over the Soviet Union is shrinking, the United States would want to redouble efforts to maintain its lead.

A U.S.-Soviet CONCOL will primarily be concerned with missions, as has the 1987 Arms Control Treaty. While the ''anti-ego'' may complain about this reduction insecurity, the ''alter ego'' would argue that reduced arms lessen the chance of war, and thus further the long-term objective of the nation to survive.

Part II

Decision-Making
for Inventions and
Innovations

5

Decision to Dare: The Foundation of Innovation CONCOLs

OVERVIEW: To resolve the conflict between improvement and innovation, a firm decision has to be made, usually involving high risks and high returns—a Decision to Dare, with a capital D.

Corporations convert the talent, training, and experience of their people—the internal capabilities—into products and services which meet external demand. What should be the appropriate ratio of innovation technology to continuation technology? When IBM decided to invent the third-generation computer system when the continuing technology was second-generation, the numerical values for the ratio could be illustrated as (99%/1% =) 99. When the number 99 is approximated to 100, it is written as 10^2, or the exponent is positive.

The resources that IBM committed to achieve the technology transformation track (3T) were a significant segment of its total. The fraction of resources committed to the potential product was significantly higher than those committed to the present products, making the resources risk ratio (3R), high (99).

The time frame of IBM's technology transformation would be intermediate, because inventing IBM 360 would take time. The combination of the 3T and 3R calibrate the Decision to Dare, the D-index. Several successful Decisions to Dare will be analyzed in the next chapter.

BETTING ON SURVIVAL

At the center of the four mission applications and the two market applications discussed in chapter 1, is the Decision to risk a significant segment of the country or corporate resources on a prespecified outcome. We capitalize the D in decision to underscore its sweep in scope and its adverse outcome. One of the most severe penalties—death—occurs when investment is made in improvement when it should have been in invention. To prevent corporate death, even in fields of preeminence, enormous risks sometimes have to be undertaken.

DECISION TO DARE ELEMENTS

By any token, the decisions we discussed in chapter 1 on missions and markets were bold ones. They committed a significant portion of total resources to a prespecified outcome. The risk was high; when you bet the company/country, you could lose it! We could call this type of decision a *Decision to Dare*.

Decision by Organism

The Decision is made by a live, human organization. Since it is made up of human beings, the organization generally produces collectively more than the sum of individual capabilities, or less than the sum, but rarely equal to the sum, depending on interaction. We use the term *organism* to acknowledge this basic interaction.

Decision to Dare

Decision to Dare is a high-risk, high-returns decision that commits a significant portion of the total resources of the organism for a prespecified outcome. We will identify three elements which help us analyze corporate/country Decision to Dare. They are: (1) technology transformation track, (2) time frame, and (3) risk ratio.

TECHNOLOGICAL TRANSFORMATION TRACK (3T)

Whether it is the IBM 360 or British radar, the corporation or the country seeks to meet external demand using internal capabilities. Being in the future, the demand is uncertain; one of several outcomes is certain, but which one is not known or even knowable.

How can the entity best meet the demand? Can it do so by doing business as usual, using the resources in the same way it has been? Or, should it change— how much, and how fast? The answer runs in terms of the *technology* base of the entity.

Technology and Hi-tech

It is useless to call technology applied knowledge or applied science. A match stick would then qualify as an instance of technology: combustion on demand— without having to rub two boy scouts together!

At the other end of the scale of energy production is nuclear fission. When the first self-sustaining nuclear reaction was demonstrated at Stagg Field at the University of Chicago on December 2, 1942, was it technology? Hardly. It was not useable technology as the match stick, but a demonstration of the feasibility of atomic technology. A fundamental feature of all technology is convenient conversion of matter into energy, matter into matter, and energy into energy. Technology is converting physical/mental, matter/energy into directly useable form(s).

What constitutes high technology (hi-tech)? It is a relative term. The Model T was high technology in its day as was the Orville brothers' flying machine. Supersonic transport is hi-tech, compared with jet transport. Our definition should take the sliding scale of technology into account, fully recognizing that the hi-tech today will become low-tech tomorrow. We could define hi-tech as multiplying manyfold the output/input ratio in converting physical/mental, matter/ energy into directly useable alternative form(s).

Transforming the Capabilities Input into Demand Outputs

The primary asset of the organism is its people. The people have capabilities— talent, training, and experience. These capabilities have to be transformed into nuts and bolts, sewing machines, and spacecraft. It is a continuing process, required of both products and processes.

Under the impetus of World War II demand, aircraft manufacturing was pushed to capacity by several corporations in the 1940s. A new technological breakthrough began to emerge in the 1950s: missiles. The corporations which survived were those which chose a sequence of technological changes—a technological transformation track—moving from all aircraft technology to some missile and some aircraft technology and to all missile technology.

Turning from products to processes, the 1960s saw several firms being transformed from aircraft into aerospace companies. An aircraft traverses its assigned path. However, in the case of the spacecraft, finding the path is as much, if not more, important than traversing it. In other words, the emphasis is on the process instead of on the product—how best to go from the suborbit to the earth orbit; from the earth orbit to the transfer orbit; from the transfer orbit to the lunar orbit; from the lunar orbit to the lunar surface; and back to the earth.

In the 1970s, the accent shifted from outer space to inner cities. The process of finding a solution methodology became more important than the solutions themselves—with an added dimension. In the case of lunar landing, the starting point is known; the goal is known; and the in-between alternative approaches are also known. However, in the case of inner city and urban problems, the starting point and the goal are far from well-defined. For instance, what is clean air? What is health? What should be the object of a national health program? What surrogate measures are acceptable to the decision makers? What is the initial value of the acceptable surrogate measure and its end-value?

Again, those aerospace corporations survived which had the foresight to move their technology profile from all aerospace to some environmental engineering and some aerospace and to all environmental engineering.

The organism uses personnel in such a way that the input of their capabilities produces the output of products/processes/services to meet the external demand. It assigns different mixes of talent to achieve different technology transformation tracks (3T).

Inertial, Improvemental, and Innovational

If the market buys what the organism produces, and keeps on buying what the organism keeps on producing the same way it has been doing in the past, we can say that there is no pressure for the organism to transform its technology. It can stay with *continuation technology*. The pressure for *invention technology* is virtually nonexistent, equal to zero percent. However, to avoid the indeterminateness of division, or by zero, we will read "0" to be "1". The ratio of invention technology/continuation technology is (1%/99%) or 0.01. The technology transformation track is 10^{-2}; the exponent is negative. We call this technology transformation track *inertial*.

Quite the opposite to the inertial was what President Haggerty of Texas Instruments (TI) perceived as the emerging demand of the market. It was for a technology quite unlike the current technology of the day, the vacuum tube. Therefore, TI decided to invent a new way of meeting the market demand—*innovational* technology transformation. The ratio invention technology/continuation technology is (99%/1%) or 99. The technology transformation track is very close to 10^2; the exponent is positive.

In between the inertial and the innovational is the *improvemental* technology transformation. The market demands that the technology be improved so that the products would be progressively changed in form and/or content. The ratio invention technology/continuation technology is (50%/50%) or 1. The technology transformation track is 10^0; the exponent is zero.

The 3T could refer to products, processes, physical activities/outputs, and/or mental activities/outputs. The output could be represented as a combination of the four: _____% product; _____% process; _____% physical; and _____% mental.

It should be remembered that when IBM chose to go for broke, as it were, to invent the 360, it had a secure market leadership position. There was no pressure to change exerted by the market. We could characterize the demand as "inertial." In other words, the mere continuation of the current technology with no appreciable change would meet the demand. However, IBM chose to risk an enormous amount of resources on an "innovational" strategy—and won.

TIME FRAME

When does the market demand that the organism employ each of these different technological transformation tracks? They could be employed in the *immediate* future, the *indefinite* future, or the *intermediate* future.

In retrospect, IBM could have held on for some time with inertial technology in the immediate future. It could probably have also bought time with improvemental technology in the intermediate future. But what IBM did was to opt for the innovational technology transformation in the immediate future.

RESOURCES RISK RATIO (3R)

Products and processes change gradually or precipitously. It is possible for the organism to concentrate on the improvemental to the exclusion of the innovational. If vacuum tubes are the present products, improvements in them will certainly satisfy the market demand for some time to come. However, if the corporation fails to prepare for the future technology of semiconductors by engaging in innovations, or acquire the new technology, then it stands to lose the future potential products by excessive focus on the present products.

Since potential products are, by definition, unproven in the marketplace, the corporation should exercise caution in abandoning the proven present products in favor of the potential products. If it were to allocate 100 percent of its resources to potential products, and 0 percent to present products, the ratio (100/0) is indeterminate. So, put "1" for "O", and obtain the large ratio of resources allocated to potential products/present products of (99/1 =) 99. If the reverse allocation holds, the ratio (1/99 =) 0.01 is small. The in-between ratio of (1/1 =) 1 is medium. The ratio of resources devoted to the potential products/present products is the resources risk ratio (3R). It can take large, medium, or small values.

We can express the ratio exponentially. The number 100 is 10^2; the number 0.01 is 10^{-2}; and the number 1 is 10^0. When the exponent is *positive* (e.g., 100 = 10^2), the organism devotes a significant amount of its resources to potential products. When the exponent is *negative*, (e.g., 0.01 = 10^{-2}), the organism devotes an insignificant amount of its resources to potential products. When the exponent is *zero*, (e.g., 1 = 10^0), the organism devotes an equal amount of its resources to potential and present products. Since the exponent calibrates the Decision to Dare, we may call it the *D-index*. The D-index can be positive, negative, or zero.

The Decision to Dare can be looked upon in terms of the technological transformation track, the time frame, and the resources risk ratio. In table 5.1, the first two are used as the rows of the matrix, and the third as the columns.

When the invention technology/continuation technology is 50%/50%, and the resources devoted to potential products and services/present products and services is 50%/50%, it is *D-zero*. The D-negative and D-positive situations can be calibrated with reference to the D-zero.

FROM ELEMENTS TO ANALYTICAL FRAMEWORK

These elements of Decision to Dare make it possible to classify innovation/improvement decisions. The D-positive, D-zero, and D-negative classifications

Table 5.1
Decision to Dare: D-Index

Resource Risk Ratio / Technological Transformation, Time Frame	Small (1% Potential Products and Services)	Medium (50% Potential Products and Services)	Large (100% Potential Products and Services)
INERTIAL (1% Invention Technology)			
Immediate	D-Negative		
Intermediate			
Indefinite			
IMPROVEMENTAL (50% Invention Technology)			
Immediate		D-Zero	
Intermediate			
Indefinite			
INNOVATIONAL (100% Invention Technology)			
Immediate			D-Positive
Intermediate			
Indefinite			

apply both to missions and markets. The type of decision determines the type of data required to move the organism to its chosen goals, measure the deviation, and take corrective steps. In other words, the D-index determines the management information systems required to provide decision support to accomplish management control. In the next chapter, we will study well-known examples of Decision to Dare in both missions and markets.

CONCLUDING OBSERVATIONS

The four high-risk, high-returns decisions pertaining to missions as well as the two pertaining to markets in chapter 1 committed significant segments of the resources of the country/corporation to uncertain outcomes, qualifying them as Decisions to Dare.

The Decision to Dare is the foundation of innovation CONCOLs. Three elements vital to the Decision were developed: the technological transformation track (3T), the time frame, and the resources risk ratio (3R).

The country/corporation has to choose a sequence of technology change: how much change, how soon? TI President Haggerty decided that to succeed in a big way, his corporation had to go all out for the invention technology of semiconductors, almost to the exclusion of the continuation technology of vacuum tubes, making the ratio invention technology/continuation technology something like $99\%/1\% = 99$, which can be approximated as 10^2, the exponent being positive.

When the technology transformation track (3T) is thus positive, it is more than likely that the ratio of the resources devoted to potential products/present products, known as resources risk ratio (3R), will also be positive.

Both the ratios can be positive, zero, or negative. The time frame in which to implement the 3T can be immediate, intermediate, or indefinite.

The Decision is characterized best by the technology transformation track and the resources risk ratio. When both are positive, the D-index is positive. The three elements and more will be incorporated into an analytic framework which will be applied to successful Decisions to Dare in the next chapter.

6

Decision to Dare: Successes in Missions (Public Sector) and Markets (Private Sector)

OVERVIEW: In this chapter, an analytical framework is developed incorporating the three elements into three factors which characterize the Decision to Dare.

The three successes documented in this chapter are: (1) the semiconductor strategy of Texas Instruments (TI); (2) the Xerox strategy of the Haloid Company; and (3) the German competition strategy of the United States. The analytical framework comprises technological gleam, marketing design, and financial risk.

Since TI President Haggerty does not tell us how he decided that developments at the structure-of-matter level would be decisive, we draw upon Bell Labs' Jack Morton who was asked to devise a plan to develop semiconductors as a viable product. Morton observes that Kelly and Shockley were making a synapse between a knowledge of need and knowledge of possibility. They had not the slightest idea what form this electronic amplification would take. But they believed that an understanding of the mechanism of electron conduction in semiconductors could lead to the synthesis of an electron device.

It is one thing to postulate a product; it is quite another to market it. Haggerty chose three "firsts" as key to his market design: (1) first silicon transistor, (2) first pocket radio, and (3) first practical integrated circuit. The financial risk involved was considerable. Haggerty risked 100 percent of the next four years' net profit to a gleam in the eye.

TI was a small good company; so was Haloid when it made the large commitment to Xerox. Haloid was seriously searching for a product: Dessauer read "every document, every publication, that might hint of a new product." Haloid committed 8.26 percent of six future years' net sales to the unknown invention.

Turning from sizeable investment for market survival to sizeable investment for national survival, we note that it was Einstein's letter to Roosevelt that provided the technological gleam that started the Manhattan Project.

Groves, the program manager, felt that scientists had little grasp of the engineering difficulties. Five different methods of production of U-235 and plutonium were pursued, because time was of the essence. The $2.19 billion spent on the Manhattan Project in four years should be compared with the army-and-navy appropriations of $1.18 billion in 1940.

Characterizing all three instances of success was the unequivocal commitment of substantial resources to products and/or processes when they were barely a technological gleam in the eye.

APPLICATIONS TO MISSIONS AND MARKETS

We will now analyze some major Decisions to Dare relating to markets and missions. The former are in the private sector, while the latter are in the public sector.

Selected Decisions

We will discuss three successes in this chapter: (1) the semiconductor strategy of Texas Instruments; (2) the Xerox strategy of the Haloid Company; and (3) the German competition strategy of the United States. In the next chapter; we will present two failures: (1) the U.S. competition strategy of Germany; and (2) the Nuvistors strategy of RCA.

Analytical Framework

We will analyze the five Decisions in terms of three factors: (1) technological gleam, (2) marketing design, and (3) financial risk.

Relation of Decision to Dare Elements and Analytical Framework

In chapter 5, we identified three elements of the Decision to Dare. How are they related to the three factors of the analytical framework?

The three elements primarily *classify*, while the three factors *characterize* the Decision to Dare. True, classification is a form of characterization. If the former is the skeletal system, the latter is the muscular system.

Thus, the technological transformation track (3T) classifies the Decision in terms of its technology content: inventive technology/continuation technology. The "technological gleam" focuses on the excitement of the invention that beckons the decision maker to untried avenues of adventure.

The resources risk ratio classifies the Decision in terms of its resources commitment: potential products and services/present products and services. The "financial risk'' focuses on the magnitude of the dollars risked today in terms of the sales, profit, and so on until the time the risk pays off.

"Marketing design" is a factor which does not have a counterpart in the three elements of classification discussed in chapter 5. The Decision to Dare is made to pursue a promising technology—not for its own sake, but for capturing a market or fulfilling a mission. Therefore, to understand what persuaded the Decision to Dare, it is imperative that the designs on and for the market/mission be examined.

MARKET APPLICATION 5: SEMICONDUCTOR STRATEGY OF TEXAS INSTRUMENTS (D-POSITIVE)

The Decision to Dare made by TI President Haggerty in 1951 was carried out during 1952–1955. The investment was substantial; the ratio of resources devoted to potential products was large. The technology transformation track was innovational. The time frame of the Decision was intermediate.

In chapter 1, we identified the Decision that Haggerty made. We will now look at elements that went into the making of that Decision.

Technological Gleam

When the transistor was invented in 1948, it was exclusively a laboratory product. It would be 15 years before the Standard Industrial Classification Manual recognized the new industry 3674—Semiconductor (solid-state) and related devices.

Betting on a Potential Process

Hardly had the invention become known when Haggerty seriously contemplated not only the *product*, the transistor, but also the *process* which would be most instrumental in advancing the future of the product:

During 1949 and 1950 it *finally became clear* to me that the future of electronics would be profoundly influenced by knowledge already attained and additional knowledge being rapidly gained about materials at the *structure-of-matter level*. . . . In early 1951 we began to formalize our strategy by definite commitment to develop, *manufacture and market semiconductor devices*. [emphasis added][1]

Of the many new ideas of the day, why did Haggerty select the rather esoteric process which could have remained a laboratory curiosity for many years to come? The phrase "finally became clear to me" suggests that Haggerty thought long and hard about the particular area of development that would enable a small company to make a decisive impact on a whole new industry yet to be born.

Elements of the Gleam

We may develop a plausible rationale for Haggety's "gleam in the eye" on semiconductors from the reflections of someone else who was involved in the basic research that led to the invention of the transistor. Jack A. Morton was provided the charter and the organization by Executive Vice President Mervin J. Kelly of Bell Laboratories. Morton recalls Kelly's motivation which suggests several important elements: current technology ceiling, unmeetable future performance requirements, and synapse between knowledge of need and knowledge of possibility:

> Mervin Kelly was aware of the *limitations* of vacuum-tube technology as long as *before the Second World War*. Kelly had been a scientist in the electron-tube field himself, and as head of Bell Labs it was important for him to *look 10 to 15 years ahead* and realize that if we had to rely on electron tubes we would *not be able to develop the more capable future communication systems* at prices anybody could afford. . . . Relays were cheap and long-lasting, but too slow. On the other hand, electron tubes were very fast. All they did was to move electrons—a very low mass—but to move those electrons you had to *pay through the nose in the hot cathode and high vacuum.* . . . How can we control those electrons?
>
> The decision to explore semiconductors was made by Kelly, but bolstered by Shockley, based on a *phenomenon of nature*: If you put the voltage in one way, you had lots of electrons: if you put it the other way, you did not. Kelly and Shockley were making a *synapse between a knowledge of need and knowledge of possibility*. They had *not the slightest idea what form* this electronic amplification would take. But they believed that an understanding of the mechanism of electron conduction in semiconductors could lead to the synthesis of an electron device. [emphasis added][2]

Imperatives to Invent

Both technological and economic limitations were pushing current technology to its useful limit. With the energy-guzzling vacuum tubes requiring "to pay through the nose in the hot cathode and high vacuum," the current technology could not support the required future developments in communications.

Invitation to Invent

The "phenomenon of nature" suggested that the flow of electrons could be controlled through semiconductors, potentially cutting the cost of moving electrons for future communication systems down. Such a new technology would make future communication systems economically viable.

Unknown Imbedding of Potential Technology

It is important to note that while the potential technology of semiconductors was reasonably postulated, Kelly and Shockley "had not the slightest idea what form this electronic amplifier would take."

If Haggerty were to retrace steps to his conclusion that structure-of-matter-level developments were the ones TI should bet on in order to capture the coming electronics market, he would probably have identified parallels to Morton's narrative.

Marketing Design

By the early 1960s, semiconductor devices would become the rage. Enticed by the prospects of quick and substantial riches, a large number of companies would flood the field so much that the "coming shakeout in electronics" would be the topic of anxious articles. But in 1949 and 1950, it was far from certain whether the transistor would even become a viable product, let alone become a versatile one. Therefore, it was imperative that a specific segment of the market which could realistically be captured be identified. Further, it had to be established that the market would make the investment viable.

Haggerty had quite specific ideas about the market for the yet-to-be-developed new product. In 1949 when TI billed net sales of $5.8 million and profits after taxes of $263,000, they defined a goal "of making TI a good big company. This was the goal we defined in 1949 as $200 million a year in net sales billed and net earnings of at least $10 million on that volume."[3]

The three products which TI selected to pursue its strategy of becoming a "good big company" were: (1) first silicon transistor, (2) first pocket radio, and (3) first practical integrated circuit. The danger of building on "firsts" is that they *may* not materialize; and if they do materialize, they may do so some place else in this case, some company other than TI. The three firsts were planned for in two semiconductor strategies:

The three principal tactics we used to fulfill our semiconductor strategy were: (1) the development of the *first silicon transistor*, (2) the development and marketing of the first pocket radio, the famous Regency, in collaboration with the IDEA Corporation, and (3) the development of our process for production of pure silicon. . . .

From this *first semiconductor strategy*, the beginning of a *second* can be traced to discussions in 1956 between Willis Adock and me in which we *speculated* on the feasibility of whole circuits processed in minute wafers of pure silicon. That *dream* became a reality with the invention of the first practical integrated circuit by Jack Kilby. . . . Jack invented the *integrated circuits* in the summer of 1958, just ten years after the invention of the transistor by Doctors Brattain and Bordeen of the Bell Telephone Laboratories. [emphasis added][4]

The hazards of building upon "firsts" are reflected in the italicized words in the foregoing quotation: *speculated, dream, first practical integrated circuit*. To look back ten years later upon the decision as having been based on a "dream" suggests the utter lack of concrete evidence on hand at the time the decision was made. The markets built upon the "dream" were therefore even more tenous.

Financial Risk

The marketing strategy was based on three new products: first silicon transistor, first pocket radio, and first practical integrated circuit. Since none of the products was marketed before, the required investment was fourfold: (1) research at the structure-of-matter level; (2) development at the transistor, integrated circuit, and pocket radio levels; (3) manufacturing for the market; and (4) marketing expenses. Even if TI succeeded in the first three investments, it could come to naught in the fourth, because the products were "firsts," completely new in form and function, making it necessary for TI to fight an uphill battle to convince the market that transistors could replace vacuum tubes; that pocket radios would perform as well as desk models; that integrated circuits would effectively replace the much larger and more cumbersome devices.

Even ignoring the investment in marketing, the outlay on research at the structure-of-matter level would be the most risky, because it would mean sunk costs with no salvage. The total investment of $4.25 million had to be committed ahead, in 1951:

The cost of carrying out this strategy for the years 1952 through 1955 was $1,250,000. This was our accumulated loss, including R&D costs for the total program, less income generated. In addition, we had committed total assets of about $3,000,000, a large proportion of which would not be salvageable if our strategy failed. Now $1,250,000 was a lot of money for us in those years. This becomes evident by comparison with our total net sales billed of $20,500,000 and net profit after taxes of $900,000 in 1952, or $28,700,000 of sales billed and $1,60,000 in profits in 1955.[5]

In retrospect, we see that the $4.25 million investment was made during four years when total sales were $97.4 million, and when total profit was $4.25 million (using the 1952 figures for 1953 and 1954 as approximations). In other words, 4.37 percent of four years' net sales and 100 percent of four years' net profits were committed to the strategy when the semiconductor was but a gleam in the eye.

MARKET APPLICATION 6: XEROX STRATEGY OF THE HALOID COMPANY (D-POSITIVE)

The Decision to Dare made by the principals of a small company in Rochester, New York, in 1946 became the industrial wonder of the mid-twentieth century: Xerox. The investment was substantial. The ratio of resources devoted to potential products was large. The technology transformation track was innovational. The time frame was immediate.

Technological Gleam

In Market Application 5, the commitment of significant resources was made on the basis of Haggerty's reasoning that the *process* that would influence electronics most significantly in the next five years and beyond would be discoveries at the structure-of-matter level. In this application, a *product*, instead of a process, is the basis of the investment.

The technological gleam in this instance was in the eye of Chester F. Carlson, who, unlike Haggerty, had no direct connection with the people who would invest in the product he would invent. A 25-line abstract on Carlon's invention published in 1945 in *Radio-Electronic Engineering* caught the attention of Dr. John H. Dessauer, a chemical engineer who left Nazi Germany for the United States, and started in 1935 with the Haloid Company, the predecessor of Xerox.

Reflecting on his 35 years with Xerox, Dessauer says that Carlson's joining the patent department of P. R. Mallory and Company was his first step toward the invention. Carlson found that drawings and specifications had to be copied for patent applications by the only available method of photostat process, which was slow and expensive. He also had another reason to seek a better method of copying in that he was developing writer's cramp, copying night after night from law books at the New York Public Library for his studies of law at night school.

Carlson believed that a source other than light could be used to create an image—such as electricity. To arrive at this hypothesis, Carlson had to explore a number of other avenues for image making:

Long evenings in the New York Public Library led Carlson to the comparatively unexplored field of photoconductivity. Was it possible that somehow *electricity, instead of light,* might be used *to make an image?* On October 22, 1938, in Astoria, Queens, with the aid of a German refuge physicist, he produced his first electrophotographic image. A 2-inch by 3-inch zinc plate was coated with sulphur, then charged electrostatically by being rubbed with a handkerchief and exposed for ten seconds to a glass slide showing the inscription "10–22–38 Astoria." The plate was dusted with lycopodium powder, which made the latent image visible, and then a piece of wax paper was pressed against the powdered image, and so imprinted with the image. To distinguish it from photography, this was called "*xerography*" (from the Greek xeros, "dry", and graphen, "to write"). [emphasis added][6]

Marketing Design

Unlike in application 5, Carlson's successful research and the development of the new product, Xerox, would *not* immediately lead to marketing a commercial product. Dessauer's book on Xerox is subtitled "The Billions Nobody Wanted." As many as 21 major corporations turned down Xerox—including IBM, General Electric, and Kodak—for six years after Carlson's invention. Even then, the support that Carlson received was limited, and by 1946, it was running out.

Haloid's Search for a New Product

Haloid was seriously searching for a new product. Dessauer disagrees with those who say that chance and luck brought Xerox Corporation into being:

I prefer to think that it was a matter of diligence. That year 1945 Joe Wilson was searching along avenues of his own, and I was reading *every document, every publication, that might hint of a new product* that the Haloid Company could market. [emphasis added][7]

"Reading every document, every publication" is indeed a dedicated effort to find a plausible new product. Why did Haloid have to look so vigorously for a new product? Because the profits were low: "In 1947 its net sales amounted to $7,062,000. After discharging all obligations, including taxes, it had a net income of only $138,000."[8]

An Ambiguous Answer from Market Research

Dessauer records that Haloid president Joe Wilson engaged a market research firm to find out if the U.S. business community *wanted* a new copying device:

The ensuing reports were not reassuring. In truth, they had an equivocal quality that was disconcerting. Before committing themselves, most people asked questions that we could not yet answer: How much would such a copier cost? How big would it be? How fast would it make copies? What would its advantage be over current methods?

But if we received no resounding "Yes!" we got no firm "No!" either. *So we went ahead.* [emphasis added][9]

Time Lapse After Invention

In application 5, the investment commitment was made to the unknown process of research at the structure-of-matter level four years before the product was invented. In this application, it was eight years after the product was invented that it found support.

Financial Risk

Dessauer recalls that the initial investment that Haloid was asked to make was $25,000—18.1 percent of net income in 1947.

Monetary Magnitude of Investment

The possibility that the investment could fail to yield a commercial success gave Haloid pause. In the meantime, the support that Carlson was receiving from Battelle Memorial Institute was running out:

It was at that time, in 1946, that Wilson and Dessauer of Haloid went to Battelle; they saw the experiments, decided that this would be their firm's new product, and invested $10,000. Within the next *six years*, Haloid raised more than *$3.5 million* to develop the process, and under the new company name of Xerox became the industrial phenomenon of the mid-century. The Xerox stock paid to Battelle in return for its royalty share in the process had a market value in 1965 of more than $355 million. [emphasis added][10]

Extent of Risk Compared to IBM's Risk

The extent of Haloid's risk in investing in Xerox was smaller than that of IBM in its 360 strategy (83 percent of four future years' total sales).

Using the base of 1947 sales of Haloid of $7,062,000,[11] the net sales in the six future years would be $42,372,000. The investment in Xerox was $3.5 million, or 8.26 percent of six future years' net sales.

Extent of Risk Compared to TI's Risk

The extent of Haloid's risk in investing in Xerox was much larger than that of TI in its semiconductor strategy (100 percent of four future years' net profits).

Using the base of Haloid's net income in 1947 of $138,000,[12] the net income in the six future years would be $828,000. The investment in Xerox was $3.5 million or 422.7 percent of six future years' net income.

MISSION APPLICATION 6: GERMAN COMPETITION STRATEGY OF UNITED STATES (D-POSITIVE)

The Decision to Dare made by President Roosevelt on October 11, 1939, was carried out during 1939–1945. The investment in men, machinery, materials, and money was unprecedented. The technology transformation track was innovational. The time frame could be considered intermediate.

Technological Gleam

In Market Application 5, TI President Haggerty made a commitment on the basis of his reasoning that a *process* would make the most important difference to the electronics industry, a commitment which he felt speeded up "by at least two years" "the entire cycle of semiconductor devices utilization in the United S'ates and the world."[13] In this application, the commitment by the U.S. president would literally change the course of war and peace in human history.

Our interest in studying the Decision to Dare is to understand the basis of such decisions, which basis enabled the undertaking of substantial risks. In Market Application 3, it was Haggerty's reasoning that the developments in structure of matter held the key to dramatic developments in electronics. In Market Application 4, it was the conviction on the part of Haloid President Wilson and Research Director Dessauer that Xerox would be their firm's new product. Dessauer showed Wilson the 25-line abstract in *Radio-Electronic Engineering:* "Of course, it's got a million miles to go before it will be marketable. But when it does become marketable, we've got to be in the picture!"[14]

The basis of President Roosevelt's decision was a letter dated August 2, 1939, written by Leo Szilard and signed by Albert Einstein.

The Uncertainty of Atomic Technology

Although Einstein signed the letter that Szilard prepared, he was uncertain about the affirmation he was making: "I did not, in fact, foresee that it would be believed that it was theoretically possible."[15] Nor was he the only one to consider the technological feasibility with skepticism. Niels Bohr concluded as many as four years after the Einstein letter: "I have, to the best of my judgment, convinced myself that in spite of all future prospects any immediate use of the latest marvelous discoveries of atomic physics is impracticable."[16]

Leslie R. Groves, Commanding General, Manhattan Engineer District, cites another important skeptic, Enrico Fermi, who would build the first atomic reactor two years later:

In general, however, it was the scientists who were personally acquainted with Hitler's New Order who first became most interested in the possible military uses of atomic energy and its effect on the existing balance of political power. . . . The group of refugee scientists in America became a focal point of the attempts to apprise officials in the federal government of the dangers and prospects that atomic physics held for the United States. Discussions of developments in this field took place between representatives of the Navy Department and Dr. George B. Pegram and *Dr. Enrico Fermi*, of Columbia, as early as March, 1939. However Fermi *expressed some skepticism* at this meeting and the United States Government did not become seriously interested until October of that year when Alexander Sachs, a Wall Street economist and a personal friend and adviser of President Roosevelt called upon him to obtain his support of the scientific research then under way. [emphasis added][17]

The Affirmative Einstein Forecast

In the light of Einstein's uncertainty and Fermi's skepticism, not to speak of Bohr's conviction that immediate uses of atomic physics discoveries were impracticable, the significance of the letter that Szilard wrote for Einstein's signature emerges vividly:

In the course of the last four months it has been made *probable*—through the work of Joliot in France was well as Fermi and Szilard in America—that it may become possible to set up nuclear chain reactions in a large mass of uranium, by which *vast amounts of power* and large quantities of new radium-like elements would be generated. Now it appears *almost certain* that this could be achieved in the *immediate future*. [emphasis added][18]

Alexander Sachs's Advocacy

Szilard heard about Alexander Sachs's fascination with atomic physics and talked with him about the possibility of alerting Roosevelt to the danger of the Nazis developing the atomic bomb first. Sachs said that he would be willing to take a letter from Einstein in person to Roosevelt if Einstein were willing to write such a letter. Sachs met with Roosevelt on October 11 and urged him to fund the project:

As the interview drew to a close, Roosevelt remarked, "Alex, what you are after is to see that the Nazis don't blow us up." Then he called Pa Watson—General Edwin M. Watson, the President's Secretary—and announced: "This requires action." Sachs left the room with Watson and by evening the Briggs Committee had been set up, a small group of men presided over by Dr. Lyman J. Briggs, director of the U.S. Bureau of Standards, charged with investigating the potentialities of nuclear fission.[19]

Unprecedented Engineering Difficulties

In assigning Groves to the Manhattan Project, the Chief of Staff, Army Services of Supply, painted a rosy picture:

The *basic research and development are done*. You just have to take the rough designs, put them into final shape, and build some plants and organize an operating force and your job will be finished and the war will be over. [emphasis added][20]

Groves was skeptical, but was not prepared for the rude awakening he was to receive as he tried to determine to what extent the Manhattan Project would be based on "real knowledge, on plausible theory or on the unproven dreams of research scientists." The basic research and development was far from complete. Recalls Groves:

I was not happy with the information I received; in fact, *I was horrified*. It seemed as if the whole endeavor was founded on possibilities rather than probabilities. Of theory there was a great deal, of proven knowledge not much. Even if the theories were correct, the *engineering difficulties would be unprecedented*. [emphasis added][21]

Marketing Design

It may appear incongruous to talk of "marketing" in connection with the atomic bomb. However, whether it is a product or service, it must have a customer. The satisfaction of a customer's need (or want) for a price is the function of marketing. As such, persuading the customer that his need (or want) is satisfied by the particular product or service is what transforms the potential use of a product or service into an actual use.

Production for Nonuse

In Market Applications 5 and 6, significant segments of corporate resources were risked to invent technologies to produce better products cheaper. The production was for *use*. The success of the marketing design is in persuading enough customers that the new products indeed best meet their needs (wants).

If the products are *not* for use, success will then be *not* in persuading customers that the products are best for use, but in persuading customers that the products are *best for nonuse*. By and large, in defense, production is for nonuse. The reasoning is that when the sufficiency of the weapons is beyond doubt by the would-be adversary, then their nonuse is beyond doubt.

Roosevelt summed up the "marketing basis" of his Manhattan Project decision when he told Sachs, "Alex, what you are after is to see that the Nazis don't blow us up." If the United States were to develop the atomic bomb before the Nazis, and the latter were convinced of that, then they would sue for peace. Groves stated the "marketing design" of Roosevelt's Decision to Dare as follows:

The basic American military requirements were twofold: to provide our armed forces with a weapon that would end the war and to do it before our enemies could use it against us. To fulfill these needs we would have to move ahead with the utmost speed.[22]

Financial Risk

At the conclusion of his meeting with Sachs, Roosevelt told his secretary, "This requires action." By that evening Sachs had help set up the Briggs Committee. The initial allocation was only $200,000 to support research on methods of production of sufficient quantities of fissionable material for an atomic bomb.

Production of U-235 and Plutonium

It was three years later (May 1942) before production of large-scale quantities of fissionable materials was deemed feasible. There were five methods—three to produce uranium, and two to produce plutonium in large quantities. Uranium production methods were electromagnetic, centrifugal, and gaseous-diffusion. Plutonium production methods were graphite reactor and heavy water reactor.

Roosevelt asked the S-1 Section—the Atomic Committee—of the Office of Scientific Research and Development (OSRD) which had on December 6, 1941, taken over from the Briggs Committee, for its recommendation on which of the five methods should be pursued. At that time the assumption was that the Germans were ahead of the United States because they had started their program in 1939, while the United States did not get under way until two years later. Therefore, the most important issue was which of the five methods would produce the fastest results. Dr. James B. Conant, President of Harvard University and Chairman of S-1 gave his estimate of the cost in his letter to Dr. Vannevar Bush, the director of OSRD:

All five methods will be entering very expensive pilot-plant development within the next six months; furthermore, if time is to be saved, the *production plants* should be under design and construction *before the pilot plant is finished*. To embark in this Napoleonic approach to the problem would require the commitment of perhaps *$500 million* and quite a mass of machinery. Anything less than this will mean either the abandonment or the slowing down of one of the methods. While all five methods now appear to be equally promising, clearly the time to production by the five routes will certainly not be the same but might vary by six months or a year. Therefore, if one discards one or two or three of the methods now, one may be *betting on the slower horse* unconsciously. [emphasis added][23]

It should be noted that time was of the essence in the critical decision. The time required for success could vary "by six months or a year." That delay could be critical. Therefore, "anything less than . . . $500 million and quite a mass of machinery" would be disastrous. The order of magnitude of the proposed investment could be appreciated by comparing it with the annual budget of Harvard University of $25 million—20 times the annual budget had to be immediately committed lest a critical three-six-month delay be incurred.

Groves assumed command of the Manhattan Project on September 17, 1942. He describes the budgeting procedure:

We were allocated funds that were already available to the War Department on an *"as required"* basis. For fiscal years 1945 and 1946, however, we had to ask for new funds. These requests were *concealed in other requests for appropriations.* During the entire period, we were allocated approximately $2,300,000,000 of which *$2,191,000,000* were expended through December 31, 1946. [emphasis added][24]

To put the Manhattan Project cost for four years in perspective, consider the appropriations for army and navy of $1,182,000 requested by Roosevelt on May 16, 1940.[25]

CONCLUDING OBSERVATIONS

In chapter 5, we developed three elements of the Decision to Dare which enable us to *classify* the Decisions. In this chapter, we developed an analytical framework which incorporates the three elements and *characterizes* the Decisions.

Three acknowledged successes were analyzed using this framework: (1) the semiconductor strategy of Texas Instruments; (2) the Xerox strategy of the Haloid Company; and (3) German competition strategy of the United States.

The three elements of the framework are technological gleam, which portrays the excitement that the invention held for the decision maker; marketing design, which portrays the designs on and for the market/mission of the decision maker; and financial risk, which portrays the magnitude of the dollars risked in terms of the sales, profits, and so on of the corporation until the break-even point.

The technological gleam beckons the decision maker well beyond the performance limits of the continuing technology. Bell Labs' Morton recognized the necessity to invent semiconductors in terms of future communications systems. Relays were cheap and long-lasting, but too slow. Electron tubes were very fast, but to move the electrons in the hot cathode and high vacuum, the cost was prohibitive. Could a way be found to move the electrons cheaply?

While Bell Labs people had no idea as to what the product would look like, Haloid's Dessauer knew that xerox was the product which they needed to survive. Inventor Carlson found that the photostatic process was cumbersome and expensive; could electricity be used, instead of light, to make good and cheap copies?

While the decision makers either already had awareness of the possible invention in a specified area in the TI and Xerox cases, the Manhattan Project invention was in the realm of "possibilities rather than probabilities. Of theory there was a great deal, of proven knowledge, not much."

While the technological gleam was a faint sputter far away, the market design was imperative. The product had to be made available immediately, if not sooner.

It may seem strange to talk about "market design" in connection with defense. Stranger still is the paradox that production in defense is for *non*use. While the atomic bomb was in fact used, the intent was to frighten the enemy into surrendering at the thought of unimaginable atrocities that would be unleashed by the new weapon.

On the other hand, semiconductors and xerox are for use. Haggerty developed his market design very carefully. He based it on several "firsts," so that TI would be the first with the most. Xerox worried time and again that others might beat them to the punch in the marketplace. They even conducted a market survey which produced equivocal results.

The financial risk in undertaking the invention and carrying out the market design was almost excessive: 423 percent of six future years' net income for the Xerox strategy of Haloid; 100 percent of four future years' net profits for the semiconductor strategy of TI; 185 percent of the combined army and navy appropriations for 1940 for the Manhattan Project.

Next we turn to two failures—in the mission and in the market.

7   *Decision to Dare: Failures in Missions (Public Sector) and Markets (Private Sector)*

OVERVIEW: Unlike the three instances of Decision to Dare in chapter 6 which were all successes, the two instances in this chapter are both failures: the U.S. competition strategy of Germany, and the Nuvistors strategy of RCA.

The analytical framework remains the same: technological gleam, marketing design, and financial risk.

"It was not her industry that had failed Germany; it was her scientists," says David Irving, who cites 16 printed pages of sources. The scientists sent a letter to the German government, predating Einstein's letter to Roosevelt. Hitler had ruled that no new weapon was to be employed until Germany had developed measures counter to it. Thus, Hitler's decision was a military decision against the atomic bomb.

CONCOLs which underlie the inability of the German scientists to exploit the technological possibility of the atomic bomb are developed. Technical considerations were outweighed by moral questions.

From the Decision *not* to dare in the public sector, we turn to the Decision *not* to Dare in the private sector.

McKinsey Director Foster calls RCA's new lines of vacuum tubes three years after IBM introduced the 360 the "sailing ship" syndrome. Sailing ships dominated sea transport in the 1850s when steamships were introduced. Scoffing at the new technology, sailing ships went from four sails to 55 by 1890, but today they carry little ocean cargo. While technological discontinuity can be postponed, it cannot be denied.

The McKinsey study suggests that as it gets close to technological limits, it gets very expensive to improve the technology. In the face of diminishing returns, RCA persisted in tinkering with an outdated technology, trying to hold off the onslaught of far more efficient semiconductors.

The failures of the German atomic bomb and of RCA's Nuvistors can be traced to the denial of significant support to powerful and promising ideas when they were not yet proven.

APPLICATIONS TO MISSIONS AND MARKETS

We continue the analysis of some major Decisions to Dare relating to missions and markets. In chapter 6, the three applications were all successes; in this chapter, the two applications are failures.

Analytical Framework

As in chapter 6, we will analyze the Decisions to Dare in terms of 3 factors: technological gleam, marketing design, and financial risk.

MISSION APPLICATION 7: U.S. COMPETITION STRATEGY OF GERMANY (D-NEGATIVE)

The Decision *not* to Dare made by Adolph Hitler on June 23, 1942, inhibited the development of the atomic bomb by Germany during 1942–1945. The investment in men, machinery, materials, and money was at best hesitant and haphazard; but it was innovational. The time frame could be considered intermediate. Since the ratio of resources devoted to potential products was small, the innovational investment should be considered D-negative.

Technological Gleam

David Irving published *The German Atomic Bomb* in 1967, making extensive use of captured German records.

Documentary and Personal Interview Basis of Evidence

Irving cites 16 printed pages of sources (pp. 305–20). The verification of major events from Irving's personal interviews is particularly impressive:

I have made use of the *entire series of German papers* at Oak Ridge: the 394 German ("G-series") nuclear research items are categorized and summarized in an excellent USAEC [U.S. Atomic Energy Commission] finding-aid, TID-3030, titled German Reports on Atomic Energy, which have now been declassified. . . .

The description of Hahn's discovery of nuclear fission is based on *my interviews* with Hahn, Strassmann and others. . . . Heisenberg's first report (December 1939) is G-39. . . . Professor Harteck's report to the War Office is in the Harteck papers: that the "special applications" he was referring to were atomic explosives was *confirmed personally to me*. . . . Hitler's decree setting up the new *Reichsforschungsrat* is in the Saur Documents, p. 6042. . . . The German thermonuclear fusion experiments are reported in . . . G-303. . . . General Groves [*Now It Can Be Told*, Harper, New York, 1962] p. 355 mentioned the rumours that the Germans were on the point of using the atomic bomb in April 1945. . . . The assessment of the German scientists' standpoint on the production of atomic bomb is based on *talks with* Heisenberg and von Weizsacker, and Heisenberg's correspondence with Bethe in 1964. [emphasis added][1]

Failure of German Scientists

The abortive attempt to make the atomic bomb is laid at the door of the German scientists by Irving:

It was not her industry that had failed Germany; it was her scientists. The manner in which they failed, during 1941, will now be seen. . . .

During a meeting in Compton's office in Chicago, a short while after the Fermi pile success [December 2, 1942], the question was posed: When might they expect the first German atomic bomb? Dr. Wigner, the most pessimistic of the group, provided on a blackboard that at least they could expect a German uranium bomb to be ready by December 1944.[2]

The German forecast was equally pessimistic. In his memoirs, *Inside the Third Reich*, Albert Speer, the master technocrat of Nazi Germany in his capacity as Minister of Armaments and War Production, recalls that he did not find the chances for a German atomic bomb hopeful at all in mid-1942:

After the lecture I asked Heisenberg how nuclear physics could be applied to the manufacture of atom bombs. His answer was by no means encouraging. He declared, to be sure, that the scientific solution had already been found and that theoretically nothing stood in the way of building such a bomb. But the technical prerequisites for production would take years to develop, two years at the earliest, even provided that the program was given maximum support. . . . [I]n any case I had been given the impression that the bomb could no longer have any bearing on the course of the war.[3]

Letter to the German Government

There is a curious parallel in the technological gleam that was in the eyes of the German scientists. They, too, sent a letter to their government, just as Einstein sent a letter to President Roosevelt. As a matter of fact, the German letter preceded the U.S. letter by four months. On April 24, 1939, Professor Paul Harteck and his assistant, Dr. William Groth, wrote a joint letter to the German War Office:

We take the liberty of calling your attention to the newest development in nuclear physics, which, in our opinion will probably make it possible to produce an explosive many orders of magnitude more powerful than any conventional ones. . . .

That country which first makes use of it has an unsurpassable advantage over the others.[4]

By the end of the month, neither Professor Harteck nor Dr. Groth had received any reply from the War Office. Their letter was passed on to Dr. Kurt Diebner, the German army expert on nuclear physics and explosives. He, in turn, consulted Professor H. Geiger, who gave his encouragement to the Harteck-Groth idea:

By the time war broke out, *Germany alone*—of all the world powers—had a *military office exclusively devoted to* the study of the military applications of *nuclear fission.* . . . There were two rival teams working on small-scale uranium research in Germany when war broke out: Diebner's and Esau's [Professor Abraham Esau, President of the Reich Bureau of Standards and head of the Physics section of the Reich Research Council of the Reich Ministry of Education]. Of these, one was shortly eliminated by the intrigues of the other. Diebner arranged an immediate secret conference to decide on the feasibility of a uranium project. . . . The first secret conference was on September 16. . . . If it were to become a question of extracting uranium-235, Otto Hahn [who on December 17 and 19, 1938 demonstrated uranium nuclear fission] now said, the project would present virtually insoluble difficulties. [emphasis added] [5]

Hitler himself was briefed on the project by Speer. Familiar with his boss's tendency to push for wild projects, Speer was very brief:

I was familiar with Hitler's tendency to push fantastic projects by making senseless demands, so that on June 23, 1942, I reported to him only very briefly on the nuclear-fission conference and what we had decided to do. . . .

Hitler had sometimes spoken to me about the possibility of an atom bomb, but the idea quite obviously strained his intellectual capacity. He was also unable to grasp the revolutionary nature of nuclear physics. In the twenty-two hundred recorded points of my conferences with Hitler, nuclear fission comes up only once, and then is mentioned with extreme brevity. Hitler did sometimes comment on its prospect, but what I told him of my conference with the physicists confirmed his view that there was not much profit in the matter. [6]

Marketing Design

We pointed out in chapter 6 that the Manhattan Project was a *political decision*. The ''customers'' would be the U.S. people who could *not* be told about the decision until the project was successfully completed, an atomic bomb was made, and dropped on target. As it turned out, Roosevelt did not make the decision to use the atomic bomb, which is when the ''customers'' emerge. So the ''market'' for the service to be rendered by the atomic bomb was the safety and survival of the United States; and the exchange value was the price of freedom from Nazi tyranny.

Since the German decision was *not* to dare, what was the ''market'' considered and rejected by Hitler? Perhaps a clue is found in the explanation he offered to Marshal Antonescu on August 5, 1944:

During a private talk with Keitel, Ribbentrop and Rumanian Marshal Antonescu, on August 5, 1944, Adolf Hitler began to talk vaguely of atomic bombs. He described Germany's latest work on ''new explosives, whose development has been advanced to the experimental stage,'' and added that in his view this one was the biggest since gunpowder. . . . The difficulty with all new weapons was the same, Hitler explained: he had ruled that no new weapon was to be employed until Germany had herself developed measures counter to it; for this reason a new type of mine they had developed could still be not employed.[7]

In other words, the "market" was the military use of the new weapon. Hitler seems to have worked on the premise that every new weapon that Germany developed would also be developed by the Allies; therefore, he considered the new weapon as being used *against* Germany, which then had to be countered. Therefore, the decision by Hitler was a military decision rather than a political one.

Financial Risk

The financial investment that the German government was willing to make on the atomic bomb project was relatively small. In retrospect, Heisenberg considers September 1941 as the time frame when he felt convinced that an atomic bomb could be made. However, within three months, the war economy was reported to be at the breaking point, which precluded large investments in any but the most dependable means of winning the war:

On December 3, Munitions Minister Fritz Todt informed Hitler that sixty armaments experts had warned that the war economy was at breaking point, and that from then on any expansion in one sector must be balanced by reduction in another. Hitler drafted and signed a decree outlining a number of clear economy measures to enable the necessary production increases elsewhere. Two days after Hitler's meeting with Todt, the director of Military Research, Professor Schumann, wrote to all the institutes working on the uranium project, warning their directors that "their work on the project undertaken by the Research Group is making demands which can be justified in the current recruiting and raw materials crisis only if there is a certainty of getting some benefit from it in the near future."[8]

It is precisely the "certainty of getting benefit in the near future" that could *not* be guaranteed. In fact, not until the spring of 1945 would the uranium pile produce fission. Therefore, in the light of a war-time economy nearing breaking point, the very scare resources would be allocated to the most promising activities, such as the Vergeltungswaffe Zwei (Revenge Weapon Two), the famous V-2. While the first V-2 was fired at London on September 7, 1944, as many as eight years earlier work had started in earnest to develop the V-2. Dr. Werner von Braun said in an interview:

Many fanciful stories have described the V-2 as part of a devilish plan devised by Hitler for use against the city of London. The real story is much less sinister and dramatic. One day, a year before Peenemunde opened [1936] [von Braun's superior, Major General

Walter] Dornberger said to me, "The Ordnance Department expects us to make a field weapon capable of carrying a large warhead over a range much beyond that of artillery. We can't hope to stay in business if we keep on firing only experimental rockets.[9]

The atomic bomb would lose the battle of the budget to other projects, such as the V-2 which had the "certainty of getting benefit in the near future." Speer says that to deploy that atomic bomb by 1945 Germany would have had to give up all other projects:

> Perhaps it would have proved possible to have the atom bomb ready for employment in 1945. But it would have meant mobilizing all our technical and financial resources to that end, as well as our scientific talent. . . .
> But even if Hitler had not had this prejudice [that the Jews were exerting a seditious influence in their concern with nuclear physics—"Jewish physics"—and the relativity theory] and even if the state of our fundamental research in June 1942 could have freed several billion instead of several million marks for the production of atom bombs, it would have been impossible—given the strain on our economic resources—to have provided the materials, priorities, and technical workers corresponding to such an investment. For it was not only superior productive capacity that allowed the United States to undertake this gigantic project. The increasing air raids had long since created an armaments emergency in Germany which ruled out any such ambitious enterprise.[10]

By March 1942, the War Office refused to pay 2 million Reichsmarks promised by General Leeb, head of German Ordnance, for nuclear research for the next financial year. The Reich Research Council was instructed to find the funds for the uranium project; and a 2-million Reichsmark budget for 1943–1944 was approved by Goring. Esau had to ask for another 1 million Reichsmarks in November 1943. For April 1944–March 1945, the budget was 3,647,000 Reichsmarks.[11] The total of some 7 million Reichsmarks, which would be less than $2 million, should be compared with the $2 billion—one thousand times as much as the German budget for the uranium project—that the Manhattan Project was allocated.

COMPARISON BETWEEN THE MANHATTAN PROJECT AND THE GERMAN URANIUM PROJECT

Technological Gleam Inspiring the Decision to Dare

It should be recalled that Roosevelt could not have made his Decision to Dare without the technological gleam in the eyes of Szilard reflected in the letter he prepared and which was signed by Einstein. It is precisely this technological promise that the German scientists were unwilling and/or unable to make.

Heisenberg felt, as of September 1941, that the atomic bomb was a technical feasibility. Just as soon as the possibility emerged, so did the associated moral questions:

Many of the physicists were by now beset with grave anxieties about the moral propriety of working on the uranium project—predominant among them being Heisenberg, von Weizsacker and Fritz Houtermans.

At the end of October, Heisenberg traveled to Denmark to see Professor Niels Bohr, to ask for his advice on the human issue. As Professor P. Jensen aptly put it, Heisenberg, the "high priest" of German theoretical physics was going to seek absolution from his Pope. Heisenberg asked the Danish physicist whether a physicist had the moral right to work on the problems of atomic bombs in war time. . . . Bohr replied that military research by physicists was inevitable everywhere and was thus proper too.[12]

The question of moral rightness with respect to the development of the atomic bomb did occur to the scientists on the Manhattan Project also. However, Einstein did not think that the release of nuclear energy would be feasible in the near future. Bohr did not think so either. Therefore, when Heisenberg spoke to him in October 1941, he was shocked to learn that Germany was on the threshold of making an atomic bomb. It could also be that the hundreds of scientists did *not* know the large projects of which their activities were all a part. Even if they had misgivings, the overriding necessity to win the war appeared to have persuaded them to work on the bomb. On the part of the German-born scientists, the burning desire to hasten the production of the atomic bomb was pronounced:

It is certainly not suggested that in not having made an atomic bomb, German scientists were morally more pure than those in America and Britain. On the other hand, as Professor Heisenberg told Professor Bethe, who had left Germany for America in the 1930's, he did not blame German emigre's for working on atomic bombs in the United States; their hate of everything German was justified, and they had to make some effort to prove their worth to their host countries.[13]

Financial Risk and Priorities

While the physicists on the Manhattan Project thought nothing of making enormous demands upon scarce resources, their German counterparts were unable to secure even limited amounts of uranium for their experiments. As early as June 1942, the uranium project scientists met with Reichsminister Speer to decide on the future of nuclear research in Germany, but they failed to inspire him. Further, even when the Reichsminister asked for the support that the scientists needed, their estimates were quite naive:

Asked by Speer how he could best help in June 1942, Heisenberg and von Weizsacker had complained that they could make no headway as they lacked the necessary building quotas: but when Speer asked how much they needed, von Weizsacker tentatively suggested the sum of about 40,000 Reichsmarks. Field-Marshall Milch recalls: "It was such a ridiculously low figure that Speer left the meetings with a negative impression of the whole uranium project; Speer told the scientists that they could have any funds they wanted, but he did not bother himself much more about the nuclear project.[14]

Concomitant Coalitions in the Development of the Atomic Bomb—German Uranium Project

In October 1942, Niels Bohr was convinced that Germany could make an atomic bomb. Why did they not?

The basic reason seems to be that the scientists did not inspire enough confidence in their government about the feasibility of making an atomic bomb. In retrospect, we can identify opposing motivations of the German scientists:

Technical Level:	*With* German success	*Against* U.S. success
Moral Level:	*Against* German success	*With* U.S. success

To the extent that the German scientists did not want to make the decision to make the bomb, or help make the decision, they were cooperating with their adversary, the United States. Such a cooperation with the adversary would be against their own government:

Moral Level: *Against* German success *With* U.S. success *Against* German government

Irving reports that Heisenberg had intended asking Bohr "whether he thought it feasible that all the scientists would agree not to direct the efforts of their governments toward the construction of atomic bombs, if he or they could be satisfied that the German physicists were also abstaining from such work"[15] Such a course of action would align the scientists against their governments:

Moral Level:	*Against* German success	*For* U.S. government
	Against U.S. success	*For* German government

If German scientists would not work toward the success of the atomic bomb, the beneficiary would be the U.S. government which would not have to contend with the powerful weapon. Similarly, if U.S. scientists would not work toward the success of the atomic bomb, the beneficiary would not have to contend with the powerful weapon. Such a step would therefore make the German and U.S. scientists allies against their governments:

German scientists	*With* U.S. scientists	*Against* German government
American scientists	*With* German scientists	*Against* U.S. government

Is science thicker than politics? Heisenberg did not raise the question with Bohr; therefore, we do not know what the answer might have been.

Concomitant Coalitions in the Use of the Atomic Bomb—U.S. Atomic Bomb Usage

If the German scientists held back their assurance of early results in the *development* of the atomic bomb, some U.S. scientists held back their support of the *use* of the atomic bomb.

Szilard, who was the moving spirit behind the Manhattan Project, stage-managing the presidential support of the project, was among the first to advocate the nonuse of the bomb once it was available.

Oppenheimer exclaimed in utter anguish in New Mexico that he had become death and destruction. Einstein was emphatically against the use of the bomb, but he did not know about its use until after the event. The upshot of all of this is that Heisenberg's ambivalence would in fact have been shared on a much a larger scale, after the bomb was made, if not before.

Szilard drew up a petition addressed to the president of the United States, urging him to give serious consideration to the moral responsibilities involved in the use of a destructive weapon of such incomparable magnitude:

First, that you exercise your power as Commander-in Chief to rule that the United States shall not resort to the use of atomic bombs in this war unless the terms which will be imposed upon Japan have been made public in detail and Japan, knowing these terms, has refused to surrender; second, that in such an event the question whether or not to use atomic bombs be decided by you in the light of the considerations presented in this petition as well as all the other moral responsibilities which are involved.[16]

Alice Kimball Smith reports that the petition (dated July 17, 1945) received 69 signatures. Szilard turned over the petition to Arthur H. Compton to transmit it to Washington through proper channels. There is no evidence that it reached the president.

The question of the use of the atomic bomb was closely connected to the future of atomic energy. It would appear that U.S. scientists were too preoccupied with the very making of the atomic bomb to give any thought to either its immediate use or eventual future.

Faced with the enormous potential for destruction, the scientists considered alternate ways of convincing the Japanese that the United States could in fact inflict unacceptable damage. The scientists for the development, but against the use of, the atomic bomb, whom we shall collectively represent by Szilard, wanted to end the war; and so did Secretary Stimson, whom we shall treat as the collective representation of top management decision makers. The CONCOL could be represented as:

Szilard *With* the United States *Against* Japan on winning the war

Stimson *With* the United States *Against* Japan on winning the war

The difference was on the use of the atomic bomb:

Szilard *With* atomic demonstration *Against* atomic destruction of Japan

Stimson *Against* atomic demonstration *With* atomic destruction of Japan

While Szilard was subsequently the arch-advocate of *demonstration*, he was the arch-advocate of *development* of the atomic bomb. Heisenberg felt that he should oppose the very development of the atomic bomb.

MARKET APPLICATION 7: NUVISTORS STRATEGY OF RCA (D-NEGATIVE)

From the Decision *not* to Dare in the public sector, we turn to the Decision *not* to Dare in the private sector.

RCA made the Decision *not* to Dare with reference to offensive R&D, opting to stay with vacuum tubes and ignore semiconductors. The investment was not substantial. The technology transformation was improvemental. The time frame of the Decision was intermediate. Since the ratio of the resources devoted to potential products was small, the Decision should be considered D-negative.

Technological Gleam

Unlike the case of the German uranium project, where thanks to Irving's pursuit of captured documents we have public records, we do not have access to RCA's hi-tech decision making. Therefore, we have to reconstruct what happened as best as we can. We know that in 1955 RCA was the leading manufacturer of vacuum tubes. By 1975 RCA was out of vacuum tubes, supplanted by the new technology of semiconductors. And RCA was out of the semiconductor business also.

The Sailing Ship Syndrome

We may characterize the persistence in linear extensions in the face of quantum jumps of technology (see chapter 4) as the sailing ship syndrome, drawing upon the fine example provided by Richard N. Foster, director of McKinsey & Co.

Foster shows how in 40 years after steamship technology was off and running, sailing ship manufacturers stuck with their technology and increased 14-fold the number of sails from 4 to 55. However, the market went past them—sailing ships carry little cargo now:

You can't stave off the inevitable economic value that can be brought from technological change.
One of the most interesting examples of this came in the ocean transport business of the 19th century. Sailing ships dominated the high seas in the 1850s. Around that time *steamships were introduced*, and sailing ship manufacturers scoffed at the new technology.

But while they did, they entered into a program of what we would now call research and development. The typical sailing ship of that time had three masts and maybe *four sails*. Within ten years it had four masts and five sails. By the 1890s we were up to seven masts with *fifty-five sails* . . . .Unfortunately, not much ocean transport is carried by sails these days. Technological discontinuity was postponed for awhile, but eventually sailing ships disappeared from the horizon. [emphasis added][17]

Nonresponsiveness to Promising New Principles

At the start of a new technology, it is quite unlikely to emerge as an efficient alternative to the established technology. The horseless carriage was roundly scoffed at for some time. While it may have been difficult to visualize it in those days, the new principle of burning a mixture of fuel and air held a potent threat to the stamina and speed of the horse as a means of transportation. So also, the new principle of controlled generation of steam held a potent threat to the stamina and speed of sailing ships as a means of transportation.

Nonresponsiveness to Market Demand

With the benefit of hindsight, we can see today that the steamship would someday replace the sailing ship. But could it have been foreseen in 1850?

If the sailing ships considered themselves to be in the sailing ship business, there was little chance. However, if they considered the true business they were in, namely, ocean transport, then the market demand for cheaper, faster ocean transportation would suggest taking a second look at the potentials of steam transportation.

In the case of vacuum tubes, the excessive consumption of electricity by them made it imperative that an alternative be found.

[A]s head of Bell Labs it was important for [Kelly] to look 10 to 15 years ahead and realize that if we had to rely on electron tubes *we would not be able to* develop the more capable future communication systems at a price anybody could *afford.* . . . To move those electrons you had to pay through the nose in the hot cathode and high vacuum. [emphasis added][18]

Faced with the prohibitive cost of moving electrons in the hot cathode and high vacuum, Bell Labs set out to find a cheaper alternative. That cost was well known to RCA and other vacuum tube manufacturers, as were the technological developments. In 1948, Brattain and Bordeen of Bell Labs invented the transistor, and in 1958, Kilby invented the first practical integrated circuit.

Furthermore, RCA knew the mushrooming of semiconductor firms in the 1960s. As a matter of fact, RCA itself was an initial entrant into semiconductors as were GE, Sylvania, and Westinghouse. Says Foster:

We have a lot of ''sailing ships'' around today. Some are called vacuum tubes. In 1968, RCA was still coming out with new lines of vacuum tubes called Nuvistors. They were *advertised as* combining *new materials, processes and functions*. Now 1968, I'll recall for you, was *three years after* IBM introduced *the 360 machine*, which had medium-scale integration, and just a year or two before they introduced the 370, which was the first large-scale integrated machine. *The electronics revolution was on and still more vacuum tubes were coming out of the laboratory.* [emphasis added][19]

Marketing Design

RCA entered the semiconductor business, but apparently its heart was not in it. Instead of concentrating on cheaper and faster electron conduction, it advertised new materials, processes, and functions in vacuum tubes in the form of Nuvistors.

In other words, it was not what the market demanded that RCA was selling; instead, it was what RCA manufactured that RCA was selling:

[RCA and other vacuum tube manufacturers were] going right back into somebody else's laboratory and generally that was another division of the same company. In this case it was RCA's black-and-white television, which went out of business a year later.[20]

RCA's marketing design to force Nuvistors down the market's throat did not succeed. And sales and profits fell.

Financial Risk

Foster tells us that the drop in market share of the leaders follows a general rule, irrespective of the particular business.

Drop in Market Share and Profits

Recalling that RCA was the leading manufacturer and enjoyed a sizeable share of the market of vacuum tubes, the McKinsey findings on how the decline and fall of market leaders across the industries allows them too little time to enter new product lines are significant:

We've looked at industry after industry and concluded that it takes between *four and seven years* for one competitor to drop from *80 percent* market share *to 20 percent* market share because of technological *dis*continuities. This is just as true in commodity chemicals as it is in semiconductors. That is *too short a time for* a company to decide to get into *a new product line*, and develop the people, skills and market reputation to be competitive.

If sales are declining in six or seven years, *profits* are probably declining to a *negative position in two to three years*. That's why NCR lost $140 million, is the reason DuPont ultimately dropped out of the tire cord business, is the reason why RCA, GE, Sylvania, and Westinghouse, all of whom were initial entrants in solid state technology, dropped out. [emphasis added][21]

Steeper Costs of Marginal Improvement

While RCA sensed that semiconductors were the upcoming technology, it continued to bet on the familiar technology of vacuum tubes, not unlike the betting on sailing ships by their owners who sensed that steamship technology was the upcoming technology.

There are inherent technological limits. When the sailing ships raised the number of sails 14-fold from 4 to 55, that was near the limit because the ships could hardly stay afloat with many more sails. The McKinsey study suggests how expensive it gets close to the technological limits:

[T]he closer you are to these limits the more expensive it becomes to improve the technology. In technological development, the economics clearly indicate diminishing returns. Our experience suggests that it is *ten times more expensive* to advance technology that is reasonably close to its limits as it is to advance one that is only half way there. [emphasis added][22]

Technology Transfer

Persistence in continuation technology in the face of the definite emergence of innovative technology extracts penalties—in market share, costs, profits, and in technology itself.

It will be recalled that RCA announced in 1958 that it planned to invest $130 million before it would earn its first dollar from color television. In a decade RCA had to import the technology. "RCA then ended up going to Japan and licensing technology for both semiconductors and color television."[23]

CONCLUDING OBSERVATIONS

The two applications in this chapter and the three in the last chapter demonstrate that the analytical framework serves us well in explaining the successes as well as the failures of hi-tech decisions of consequence, in both the public and the private sectors.

In chapter 6, we developed an analytical framework comprising three elements: technological gleam, which portrays the excitement that the invention holds for the decision maker; marketing design, which portrays the designs on and for the market/mission of the decision maker; and financial risk, which portrays the magnitude of the dollars risked in terms of the sales, profits, and so on, of the corporation until the break-even point.

We saw from the detailed case study of the German atomic bomb that technological gleam was conspicuous by its absence. Albert Speer, the Minister of Armaments and War Productions, recalled that in mid-1942 Heisenberg's answer gave him "the impression that the bomb could no longer have any bearing on the course of the war." Speer mentioned nuclear fusion only once in the 2200 recorded points of his conferences with Hitler; and that was to confirm Hitler's view that "there was not much profit in the matter."

The "market" for the "product" was quite different in Germany from what it was in the United States. While Roosevelt took a political decision in behalf of the United States to produce the product, Hitler took a military decision not to proceed with the atomic bomb until Germany developed an effective countermeasure.

With virtually no technological gleam, and no identified market, the financial risk that the German government was willing to make on the atomic project was relatively small. The atomic bomb project would lose out to the V-2 which had the "certainty of getting benefit in the near future." The total of some 7 million Reichsmarks (less than \$2 million) should be compared with \$2 billion for the Manhattan Project, which was one thousand times as much as the German budget.

Turning from the Decision not to Dare in the public sector to the Decision not to Dare in the private sector, we characterized RCA's clinging to "linear extensions" in the face of "quantum jumps" of technology as the sailing ship syndrome, after Richard N. Foster of McKinsey & Co., who described how sailing ships kept increasing the number of sails from 4 to 55 in the face of steamship technology.

The excessive consumption of energy by the vacuum tubes made it imperative that an alternative technology be found. Yet three years after IBM introduced the 360 with medium-scale integration, RCA, an early entrant into semiconductors was bringing out new lines of vacuum tubes called Nuvistors. RCA's market design was to sell Nuvistors, not to outsiders, but to other divisions of RCA. The drop in market share, and the steeper drop in profits, should have clanged loud bells of warning to RCA on its financial risk.

Of the three elements of the analytical framework, the technological gleam is the necessary, though not the sufficient, condition for the Decision to Dare. Since the decision maker must have the assurance of a technological base from which to mount his invasion of the market, we turn now to the methods of technology forecasting which provide the profile, however sketchy and uncertain, of the technological prospects which invite the Decision to Dare.

Part III

Forecasting Inventions and Innovations

8

Technology Requirements and Feasibility Forecasts

OVERVIEW: A critical factor in the dramatic failure of RCA and the dramatic success of TI in semiconductors was the dependable forecast of technology, or the lack of it. TI's Haggerty not only foresaw that coming developments at the structure-of-matter level would profoundly affect the future, but also made a commitment to that future, while RCA clung to vacuum tubes.

It is one thing to select a technology area; it is quite another to specify the profile of the product(s) that should be made in that area. Who should do the specification: user (market-pull) or inventor (technology-push)? The NSF study on innovations supports the former, while the Arthur D. Little (ADL) study supports the latter.

To forecast linear extensions of the properties of the product, continuities methods, such as linear regression, are appropriate. To forecast quantum jumps, discontinuities methods, such as relevance tree, are appropriate.

Using the McKinsey study of Du Pont's avoidable investment of $40 million in R&D for nylon cord tire, we find that points of inflection of performance characteristics, market share, and profits are crucial elements in sound R&D investment decisions.

THE DECISION: IMPROVE A PRESENT PRODUCT, OR INVENT A NEW ONE?

In chapter 3 we discussed dramatic instances of failure and success: RCA opting to stay with vacuum tubes, ignoring semiconductors (amplified in chapter 7); Texas Instruments gambling its future on hopes of future knowledge at the "structure-of-matter" level (amplified in chapter 1).

Banking on the Unknown

It is one thing to make a "do-or-die" gamble; it is quite another to make it a way of life. TRW stated its philosophy of gambling everything on technology on a continuing basis when it said in 1961 that in the coming decade about two-thirds of its sales would come from products which were then not even on the drawing board.

In terms of the N/M ratio, TRW's target N is 2/3; therefore M is 1/3. The N/M ratio is ($2/3 \times 3/1 =$) 2. When the value of the ratio is 1, the offensive R&D equals defensive R&D; when it is less than 1, recall the epitaphs in chapter 3!

Corporate Choice of Technology Areas

How does a coroporation choose to live dangerously? It is not enough if the corporation (agency) decides that more than half its future revenue should come from products yet to be invented. It should also specify the areas of technology wherein the new products should be found. TRW which met and exceeded in 1967 its announced goal in 1961 of becoming a billion-dollar company before the decade was out, specified the six technology areas of such a billion-dollar company in 1968: (1) the use of *systems engineering* techniques to solve problems such as environmental pollution and urban development; (2) research and development activities ranging from new advances in *life sciences and materials technology* to new control systems for the petroleum industry; (3) new *unmanned spacecraft programs* involving navigation control, earth resources, and advanced communications satellites; (4) new concepts for high-speed *ground transportation*, representing one of many potential growth areas in the field of civil systems; (5) greater demand for *microelectronics circuitry* in commercial and government markets; (6) *information systems and computer software* services, which continue to contribute importantly to TRW's growth. [emphasis added][1]

The choice of technology areas is essential not only for markets but also for missions. In chapter 4 we identified 20 basic technology areas which DOD considers crucial to the future weapon systems, a list updated and published each year since 1979.

Technology areas are generic. TRW would not want to specify the particular linear extension or quantum jumps it focuses on, because that would be tipping its hand, inviting the competition to explore the specific technology area, and even to beat TRW.

THE INSPIRATION: IMPETUS TO INVENTION—FROM USER OR INVENTOR?

The corporation (agency) can choose specific technology areas in which it might improve or invent products. To calibrate advances in improvement/invention, it is essential to specify the profile of the end-product itself, or at least how different the improved/invented product would be from the present one. Who should specify this? How should the specification be made?

There are two schools of thought on the subject. One holds that the user should specify need. Another holds that the inventor should specify what should (could) be invented. Texas Instruments President Haggerty goes one step further: "But believe me, in those cases where R&D is the key, I, as Chief Executive of TI must receive *not just information, but inspiration, from those in our management responsible at top levels for the R&D* direction of this company" (emphasis added).[2]

Notice that Haggerty is asking R&D managers, not marketing managers, not only to inform him, but also to inspire him on the new products. We will explore first the opposite point of view, which asks the external demand (user) to specify the profile of the new product, instead of the internal supply (inventor).

THE SPECIFICATION OF TECHNOLOGICAL CHARACTERISTICS BY USER

To develop a new product, it first has to be specified. What will the new product do? That specification has to be in terms of the performance characteristics of the product to be invented (improved). Who should specify these performance characteristics?

Project Hindsight

Project Hindsight (1967) undertook a most extensive study of the past history of weapons systems development, underscoring the role of defense need:

> The need orientation factor was studied in depth because it was so obviously relevant to the matter of uniqueness of the DOD's need for knowledge. For example, the performers of the RXD Research or Exploratory Development *Events*, or their immediate supervisors were asked: "What was the objective of the work?" or "What led you into this area of research?" . . . Most significant of the results of an analysis of their answers is the fact that, in the case of both science and technology, *a DOD need was usually cited as the motivational factor.* . . .
>
> The *Event* is simply the birth of new or important scientific or technical information, or the synthesis of information into an important new technological capability. . . . The twenty systems studied contributed a total of 835 analyzed Events of which 710 were distinct; i.e., 125 Events were identified in more than one system. [emphasis added][3]

NSF Study of Innovation

Since DOD is the prime customer of weapon systems, DOD need is the "market-pull" Factor. This factor is rated as the second highest among "21 factors of probable importance to the direction and rate of the innovative process

... selected from the general literature" in the 1968 National Science Foundation study of 533 significant events in ten innovations. The highest factor, "Recognition of Technical Opportunity," was judged moderately or highly important in 87 percent of decisive events; and the "Recognition of the Need" in 69 percent. Concludes the NSF study: "Ranking second is Recognition of the Need, which is closely akin to what is sometimes called '*market pull*' " (emphasis added).[4]

THE SPECIFICATION OF TECHNOLOGICAL CHARACTERISTICS BY INVENTOR

In 1986 Arthur D. Little Inc. (ADL) published an international study of 12 innovations, ranging from VCRs to Nautilus machines, and from Federal Express to the CAT scan. It refutes the market-pull thesis.

ADL Study

The study focuses on breakthroughs—quantum jumps:

Innovation, as we came to understand it in our breakthroughs research, is the art of doing the same thing you are doing now but doing it better. A breakthrough is the act of doing something so different that it cannot be compared to any existing practices or perceptions.

We cite here for comparison Haggerty whose breakthrough strategy catapulted the $20-million TI to a multibillion-dollar level:

If an innovative effort is to be of such significance that, if it succeeds, it really will have a major impact on a big company—a real *breakthrough strategy* [the sort of *single strategy*, the success of which can produce *10% growth rates per year all by itself*, even in a large corporation]—then at some critical time in its development the risk will be very large (Haggerty, interview, 31; emphasis added).

It is true that no breakthrough becomes commercial unless the people developing it see a market for it. But it is flatly wrong—though we have encountered this assertion frequently—to say that the bulk of successful commercial innovation results from "market pull" rather than "technology push." That is a topsy-turvey analysis—it expresses the *outcome* of a new idea as its *origin*.

In discussions with sixteen companies involved in getting a dozen commercial breakthroughs under way, we asked specifically what was the motivating force—what *really* got the idea going at the very beginning. We focused not on the beginning of the product development, but on the *concept* that preceded the development. In every case, in all sixteen, it was "technology push"—more accurately, it was the *curiosity* within the originating person—that lit the fire. Neither financial need nor market intelligence played a major role in these exceptional beginnings. [emphasis added][5]

It is important to note that in every case, in all sixteen, it was "technology push," or a case of 100 percent "technology push".

In contrast, Project Hindsight found that DOD need was critical to invention. We saw in chapter 1 that Churchill found the defense need critical to the invention of radar: ''My experience is that in these matters, when the need is fully explained by the military and political authorities, Science is always able to provide something.''

While these two are instances of military need, the ten inventions in the NSF study, ranging from hybrid grains to video tape recorders, were predominantly nonmilitary. Yet 69 percent of the decisive events—especially important occurrences that provide a major and essential impetus to the innovation—rated ''market-pull'' moderately or highly important.

Role of the Technical Entrepreneur

While the NSF and ADL studies differ on the prime impulse to innovation, they seem to recognize the need for a champion.

The NSF study refers to a *technical entrepreneur*—an individual within the organization who champions a scientific or technical activity; he is sometimes also called a ''product champion.'' In nine out of the ten innovations, the technical entrepreneur was cited as important. ''This is the strongest conclusion that emerges from the study. . . . If any suggestion were to be made as to what should be done to promote innovation, it would be to find—if one can—technical entrepreneurs.''[6]

The ADL study does not use the term *technical entrepreneur*, but does recognize a championing role for management:

But there are in fact, management actions that have fostered breakthroughs. They happened at Montedison, Toyota, Raytheon, and several other of the breakthrough companies in this book. However, these actions fall more accurately in the realm of ''responsiveness'' rather than under the heading of ''management.''

When successful breakthrough managers finally stepped in and involved themselves in a project that was already well advanced, their role was to serve as ''sword and shield.'' They shielded the team, and fenced with the Establishment. . . . Italo Trapasso stated the only effective philosophy for a breakthrough manager when he said, ''I was kind of a servant to them. I was their assistant.''[7]

THE FORECAST: TYPES OF METHODS

Whether invention is user-driven or inventor-driven, dependable technological forecasts are essential to the corporate (agency) commitment of resources to a change in the performance characteristics of products—linear extensions or quantum jumps.

Forecasting Linear Extensions

If the new product requires only the linear extension of present behavioral properties, then methods which fore (front) cast (throw)—throw the past to the future—would be appropriate. The different methods are variations on the theme that future is past extended. We may term these as "extension methods," or "continuities methods" because they are based on continuation of the present.

Forecasting Quantum Jumps

Methods that postulate the continuance of the present cannot help predict discontinuities of the present. That was why the automobile was not invented by the farmer breeding faster race horses, nor was the airplane invented by the railroad manufacturer building faster railroad engines. The methods that predict horseless carriages when only horse carriages are around, and railless roads when only railroads are around, merit the name *discontinuities methods*.

Exploratory and Normative Methods

In 1967, Erich Jantsch published a number of forecasting methods in *Technological Forecasting* (OECD, Paris, 1967). He defined a group of extrapolative techniques as "exploratory."

For what we call quantum jumps, Jantsch's "normative methods" would also be appropriate. They determine the future through goal setting and resource allocation.

Illustrative Continuities Methods

Different technological forecasting methods are described in the literature (e.g., Joseph P. Martino, *Technological Forecasting for Decision-Making*, North-Holland, Amsterdam, 1983). Our purpose here is to indicate how choices may be made between different methods.

New products based on linear extensions of the performance characteristics of present products would call for continuities methods. The simplest of these is the linear model, which says that performance characteristics increase with time (or another variable[s]).

The increase could be a constant percentage. Or it could be exponential, the rate of increase itself increasing or decreasing.

Growth has to stop sometime. It occurs when the performance characteristics have reached maturity, increase being zero. When will maturity occur? It depends on the shape of the particular curve.

Growth analogies identify a phenomenon parallel to the one under study. Since the historical parallel traced a given path, a similar path is forecast for the new product under study.

Certain developments require certain prerequisites, the progress in which could be studied to forecast the progress in the behavioral properties of interest.

Physical limits set the upper limits of performance characteristics. While continuities methods will forecast the progress up to the barrier, discontinuities methods are required to set the performance characteristics beyond the barrier, and then to assess the prospects of ever reaching those future dimensions.

Illustrative Discontinuance Methods

The "normative" methods run in terms of "ought" propositions. To solve a given problem, such-and-such "ought" to be done. These can be stated in terms of the requirements: such-and-such ought to perform thus-and-so.

We can use morphological models to determine the (maximum) number of possible solutions to a given problem. Using Fritz Zwicky's methods introduced in *Morphology of Propulsive Power* (California Institute of Technology Bookstore, Pasadena, 1962), we can break up the problem (e.g., automobile propulsion) into parallel parts, such as the number of wheels (4), the number of engines (4), the type of engines (3), the type of transmission (2), and the type of power sources (5), yielding a total of 4 x 4 x 3 x 2 x 5 = 480 possible solutions. To be useful, these parallel parts must be comprehensive, so that all possible solutions can be identified. After removing the impossible solutions, the performance characteristics of each element can be derived for each solution.

Another normative method is the relevance tree. It breaks up a problem into hierarchical parts instead of parallel parts (as in morphological models).

Planning Assistance Through Technical Evaluation of Relevance Numbers (PATTERN) is a relevance tree technique which Honeywell uses to select long-range R&D investment programs:

PATTERN used in the military areas can best be described as a decision aid consisting of three basic parts: first, a Relevance Tree which measures the relative importance to national objectives by upgrading a particular mission or technical area; second, Cross Support which measures the degree of technical growth that will result from solving a specific problem; and third, Status and Timing which measures industry's capability to solve identified technical problems. A scenario which projects the world environment (including military, political, and economical factors) that might be expected in the next decade and a state-of-the-art technology assessment are used as basic inputs in the evaluation process.

At each node of the tree, a team of experts, using matrices, decision criteria, and subjective probability assign quantitative values relating to the relative importance of upgrading that item in terms of its contribution to meeting the overall national objectives for the next decade.[8]

Empirical Development of Selection Criteria

We will now examine a market application of R&D investment in a product which cost the investor an avoidable $40 million. What should the investor have required of forecasting methods to avoid the mistake? This real-life marketing application gives us the basis to develop criteria for selection of forecasting methods.

MARKET APPLICATION 8: "DU PONT [LOST OUT] BECAUSE IT IMPLICITLY ASSUMED THAT . . . IT COULD CONTROL THE PACE OF INNOVATION IN THE MARKETPLACE. IT COULDN'T"

We will draw upon the narrative of McKinsey & Co. director Richard Foster in his book *Innovation–The Attacker's Advantage* on the telltale signs of Du Pont's declining rate of returns on R&D in tire cord.

Performance Characteristics

The performance characteristics of the tire cord includes: cord strength, heat stability, adhesion, and fatigue. Together they give tires the properties desired by the customers: a smooth ride, endurance, blowout protection, and low cost.

Baseline Measure of Performance

Foster chose the first tire-cord fiber, cotton, as the yardstick. He gave the value *1* to the best performance of cotton tire cord.

Successive Measures of Performance

The first synthetic tire cord was rayon. It did not rot like cotton; and tires made from rayon had a much longer life. Rayon tire cord earned a value slightly higher than 1 for relative cord performance.

Performance Returns for R&D Investment

R&D Investment	Improvement in Performance	P/R&D
First $60 million	800%	13.3
Next $15 million	25%	1.7
Final $25 million	5%	0.2

Three "S-Curves"

Foster observes that a significant portion of the $40 million spent after 1962 might have been saved if limits had been understood.

After World War II, Du Pont switched from rayon to its proprietary nylon

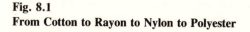

Fig. 8.1
From Cotton to Rayon to Nylon to Polyester

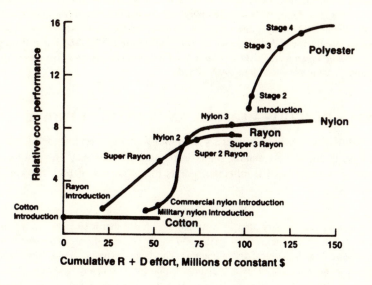

DuPont, not understanding where nylon was on its S-curve, got little for its last $75 million of R&D, while Celanese progressed much faster with less money because polyester was just starting its curve.

Source: Richard Foster, *Innovation—The Attacker's Advantage*, Simon & Schuster, New York, 1986, p. 124.

tire cord. When the nylon tires developed "flat spots" due to the tires freezing when the car was parked for a while on cold winter days, the tire manufacturers wanted to try polyester as an alternative to nylon.

Foster draws an "s-curve" for each of the three technologies—rayon, nylon, and polyester—which are reproduced in Figure 8.1. He points out that the physical limits of relative performance for nylon were 8, while those for polyester were twice as high (at about 16):

Du Pont embarked on a dual approach. It pursued substitute polymers like polyester but also tried to improve nylon's flexibility to get rid of flat spots. *Unfortunately Du Pont didn't know where nylon was on its S-curve.* That lack of information proved costly. *Nylon was closer to the limits of its technological potential than anyone had guessed.* Lots of money poured into R&D could not, in fact *did not, make much of a difference.* [emphasis added][9]

Quite the opposite was the case of polyester. Celanese captured its advantage of a physical limit twice that of Du Pont's nylon:

Polyester was still in its adolescence. *Celanese's adolescent polyester technology had a 5-to-1 advantage over Du Pont's mature nylon technology.* . . . [T]here was an increase in the steepness of the S-curve from one generation of technology to the next, and polyester had much higher limits. The *polyester limits were about 16* on the performance chart *versus 8 for nylon.* Once perfected, the polyester corded tire would last longer and stay more flexible at lower temperatures—no flat spots—than the very best nylon-corded tire.

Celanese could spend *half* as much *as Du Pont* on tire cord *R&D*, but still progress *two-and-a-half times faster* than Du Pont since its *productivity was five times higher.* Less money, more progress. [emphasis added][10]

FINANCE OUTCOME MEASURE: RM/IR RATIO OF PROFIT

The McKinsey study of America's technology leaders who lost their leadership gives results about their market share drop and profit decline. The results seem to warrant our looking for inflection points in the curves of both market share and profits:

We've looked at industry after industry and concluded that it takes between *four and seven years* for one competitor to drop from *80 percent market share to 20 percent* market share because of technological discontinuities. This is just as true in *commodity chemicals* as it is in *semiconductors.* This is too short a time for a company to decide to get into a new product line, and develop the people, skills and market reputation to be competitive.

If sales are declining in six or seven years, *profits* are probably declining *to a negative position in two to three years.* That's why NCR lost $140 million, is the reason Du Pont ultimately dropped out of the tire cord business, is the reason why RCA, GE, Sylvania, and Westinghouse, all of whom were initial entrants in solid state technology, dropped out. [emphasis added][11]

A 60 percent drop in market share in four to seven years works out to 9 to 15 percent average per year. In reality, the drop will more likely be uneven. So, a drop in market share by nine percent in year 1, followed by another drop of 12 percent in year 2, could be considered as the point of inflection from rapid growth to maturity—or rather, from maturity to decline. Barring other evidence to the contrary, if the corporation were to take remedial action in year 3, it would have at least one, and at most four years to salvage its sales and profits.

CONCLUDING OBSERVATIONS

To reduce the risk of sticking to an obsolete technology, a corporation must first identify its areas of strength. Profiles of new products in these areas have to be specified, either by the user (market-pull) or the inventor (technology-push). The NSF study on invention favors the former, while the ADL study the latter.

Whether the invention is user-driven or inventor-driven, dependable forecasts of technology are critical. If the new product requires only linear extensions, continuities methods forecasts (such as linear regression) would be appropriate; if it requires quantum jumps, discontinuities methods (such as relevance tree) would be useful.

The McKinsey study shows that Du Pont could have saved $40 million in R&D investment. One strong conclusion we can draw is that the points of inflection of performance characteristics, market share, and profits are critical. We turn next to a new method which recomputes the growth stage of the data set with every new data point.

9

MESGRO Forecasting for Technology and Territory

OVERVIEW: Anticipating the coming change in the direction of the technology curve (e.g., performance characteristics of a product) can make a world of difference to the technology manager. If he finds that the improvement in results corresponding to increase in efforts is decreasing, or increasing at a decreasing rate, he should seriously consider alternate technology areas to explore.

Stages of growth are recomputed with each new data point by a new computer-based numerical forecasting algorithm called MESGRO (Modified Exponential Smoothing-GROwth).

Making no assumptions about the nature of the data, MESGRO learns the structure of the data series by successively forecasting the third point from the first two, the fourth point from the first three, the fifth data point from the first four, and so on. To come as close to the given point, the fifth data point, from the first four, MESGRO splits the data into two parts: recent and remote. With four data points, the "recent" can be data point 4, and the "remote" data points 1, 2, and 3. Or, the "recent" could consist of data points 4 and 3, and the "remote" data points 1 and 2. Or the "recent" could be data points 4, 3, and 2, and the "remote," data point 1.

"Recent" is given the weight of .9, "remote" $(1 - .9 =) .1$; or "recent" is given the weight of 0.85, "remote" receiving 0.15. That set of values is chosen for "recent" and "remote" which makes the forecast of fifth data point come closest to the actual.

MESGRO is found to be very sensitive to changes in data, as shown by its identification of the growth stage of the chemical sales data changing from rapid growth to maturity to decline with each new data point added in period 7, 8, and 9.

Such sensitivity can be vital to anticipating coming changes in the growth curve, whether of technology or territory. MESGRO also provides macro-forecasts, using large chunks of data to assess the long-term trends in technology and territory.

Why should MESGRO forecast be trusted? It studies the first half of the given data to forecast the second half. Individual data points, instead of their average, are used to determine how closely MESGRO fits the actuals. MESGRO's accuracy makes it suitable for control purposes.

MESGRO fits the model to the data instead of data to the model, so that the manager can control outcome by design, instead of by default.

NEEDED: HIGHLY ACCURATE ADAPTIVE FORECASTS FROM FEW DATA POINTS

Enormous stakes ride on dependable forecasts of the points of inflection in technological, market, and profit curves. The anticipation of turning points requires an approach which can identify growth stages and asymptotes. Further, the approach should quickly adapt to fluctuations, making changes to the forecasts giving unequal weights to data points. When a single data point suddenly appears out of step with the preceding points, how much weight should it be given? This issue is particularly important in technological breakthroughs. We will examine these different features with respect to a new numerical forecasting method called Modified Exponential Smoothing-GROwth (MESGRO).

MESGRO has been successfully applied to over 45 real-life applications in widely ranging fields, from consumer product sales to weapons acquisition programs, from new housing construction to fertilizer prices, and from R&D projects to manufacturing programs. MESGRO won a U.S. National Science Foundation competitive award for International Scientific Lectures.

The future is uncertain. That does not mean that we do not know anything about it—we know some things. But no forecast is error-free. Reduction of error—the difference between the actual and the forecast—is what forecasts strive for. Since reduction of error costs money, we have to determine how sensitive decisions are to error.

Forecast Feature 1: Accuracy Instead of Inaccuracy

It may sound strange that any forecast would aim at inaccuracy. But almost all forecasts do.

Procrustus, the robber-son of Poseidon in Greek mythology, offered his bed to weary travelers. If the traveler was too tall for the bed, Procrustus would cut him down to size to fit; if too short, Procrustus stretched him until he did fit. In either case, the traveler was made to fit.

Like Procrustus, we often insist that given data conform to a linear model in monthly sales increase or decrease by exactly the same amount. If the rate of increase is three hundred units, then sales for the second month will be three hundred units more than the first month. Sales in the third month will be six

Fig. 9.1
Observed Data for 24 Time Periods

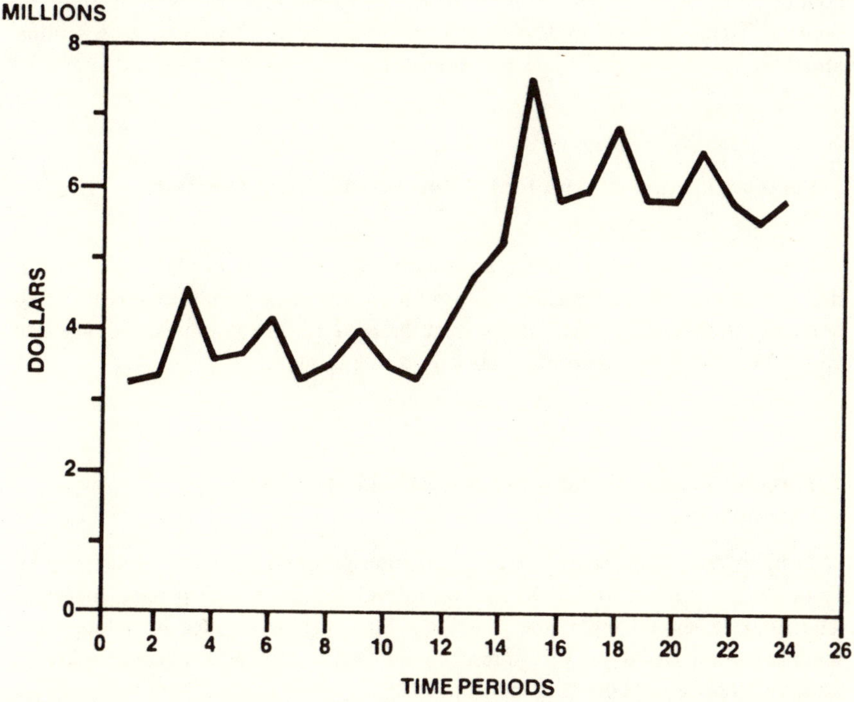

hundred units more than the first; and the tenth month nine hundred more than the first.

How is this uniform rate of increase or decrease determined? By selecting, from all possible rates, that particular rate which gives forecasts that are wrong in a special way. In a month when sales are 393 units and the forecast 490, the error (actual minus forecast) is −97. In other months, the quantity could be positive. The mathematics of arriving at a particular rate of uniform increase or decrease balances a measure based on these positive and negative values of error.

The objective of the linear fit is not to make a single accurate forecast, but to forecast all points inaccurately. The method balances errors on both sides. The old joke about a statistician—someone with his head in boiling water and feet in ice, but on the average comfortable—is perhaps not without justification.

Such inaccuracy is, however, intolerable to program managers of U.S. defense systems acquisition programs, which, on the average cost over $2.5 billion. A small segment could exceed $100 million. When the actual is $100 million and the forecast is only 10 percent in error, the quantity (actual minus forecast) is 100 minus 90, or 110 minus 100.

It is possible to forecast 90 when the actual is 110, making the error $20 million. At 20 percent interest per year (in 1979 the prime interest rate was 21 percent), the borrowing or avoidable holding of $10 million costs $166,667 more per month. One program manager of a vital component in a major acquisition confided that he considers himself lucky when the forecast error is only 13 percent! That is a range of $26 million on a base of $100 million, representing an additional cost of $433,333 per month. Error is indeed expensive!

Forecast Feature 2: Accuracy Achieved with Very Few Data Points

In major systems acquisitions, as in early sales of a new product, it is critical that forecasts achieve high accuracy with as few data points as possible. To demand 50 or 60 data points to forecast the next 12 data points is a luxury few can afford. Decisions have to be based on scanty data.

Forecast Feature 3: Adaptive Adjustments to Violent Fluctuations

In figure 9.1, data for a systems acquisition program registers a sudden jump from $5.219 million to $7.545 million in one month, a 44.5 percent increase! The forecast should tell if the jump is a one-time occurrence or a long-term tendency, and based on that inference the forecast should adjust quickly to structural changes in the data environment.

Forecast Feature 4: Self-validation, Instead of Open-ended Error Equivalence

Linear and nonlinear forecasts steer clear of accuracy of individual data points. This is not the fault of computations; it is inherent in the concept. When a straight line minimizing the measure of errors is drawn through given data points, the forecast suggests that future data will almost always be either higher or lower than individual forecasts, but the errors will be about equal.

If the first three forecasts underestimate the actual, chances are the next three may overestimate. The program manager has spent $500,000 of borrowed money to run the program in the first three months, and then is told in the next three months he could pile up excess funds saving $500,000 in interest—if only he knew in advance when to borrow and when not to borrow. His management will not be assessed with "zero" error, but with a $1-million error!

If instead, he had a forecasting method which validates the accuracy on already available data, that could lend credence to his capability of forecasting in reasonably accurate fashion.

Fig. 9.2
MESGRO Forecast of 25th Time Period

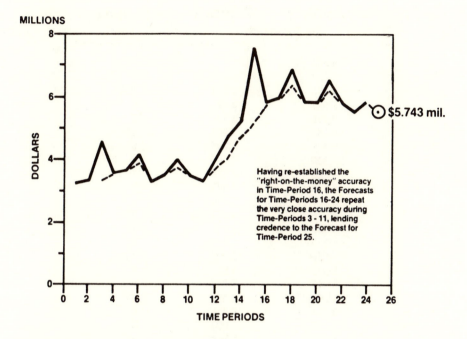

MILLIONS

Having re-established the
"right-on-the-money" accuracy
in Time-Period 16, the Forecasts
for Time-Periods 16-24 repeat
the very close accuracy during
Time-Periods 3 - 11, lending
credence to the Forecast for
Time-Period 25.

$5.743 mil.

DOLLARS

TIME PERIODS

MESGRO METHOD AND FEATURES

MESGRO incorporates all four desirable features of forecasts for decision making. Further, it recomputes the stage of growth with addition of each new data point.

MESGRO Feature 1: Accent on Accuracy—Short Term

Instead of force fitting data to a preconceived model, MESGRO discovers the structure of given data. It does so for both short-term and long-term data.

In the short term, MESGRO starts with data points 1 and 2, and asks how these two data points should be combined to obtain data point 3. Once data point 3 is forecast, the difference (actual minus forecast) is calculated. Now, given data points 1, 2, and 3, and the error of data point 3 forecast, how can data points 1, 2, and 3 be combined to obtain data point 4? The error is again calculated, this time for data point 4, and so on.

Experience with over 45 real-life data series shows that MESGRO is able to track data structure by the third forecast, with error decreasing rapidly toward zero by data point 5.

Table 9.1
MESGRO Forecast Versus Actual Data

Actual	Forecast	Fit Index
(In Thousands $)		
3,241		
3,327		
4,556	3,326	454
3,552	3,551	0
3,636	3,636	0
4,160	3,908	16
3,295	3,295	0
3,500	3,500	0
4,025	3,778	16
3,512	3,513	0
3,337	3,338	0
4,076	3,743	29
4,802	4,071	131
5,219	4,790	38
7,545	5,204	1,052
5,835	5,833	0
5,948	5,956	0
6,863	6,417	31
5,835	5,838	0
5,828	5,823	0
6,552	6,284	11
5,807	5,806	0
5,530	5,529	0
5,869	5,868	0

MESGRO Feature 2: Accent on Accuracy—Long Term

Instead of the data's microstructure—how data point 2 is connected to data points 3 and 4, one step at a time—the long-run MESGRO studies the data's microstructure.

Taking points 15, 24, 39, or whatever the number of available data points as a whole, is it reasonable to consider the data as exhibiting one segment, two segments, three, or more? How much weight should be given to each segment?

As in the short run, long-run forecasts are also checked against actuals. Data are divided into two parts, the first half used to forecast the second. Three forecasts—call them red, blue, and green, to avoid suggestion of superiority as in first, second, and third forecasts—are made for the latter half of the data.

How close is the MESGRO forecast? Experience with a large number of data sets has shown one of the three forecasts—red, blue or green—always fits the data best. But which one?

Fig. 9.3
Stages of Growth

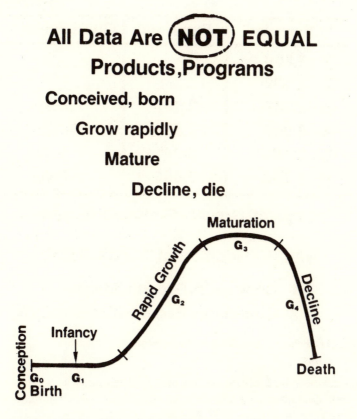

Suppose data for 24 months are available. We use the first 12 months to determine three forecasts of months 13 to 24. Divide the actual for month 13 by the red forecast for month 13. Ideally, the ratio will be 1, or 100 percent. For month 13 let us say the values are 98.9 percent for red, 100.1 percent for blue, and 100.9 percent for green. The closest to 100 percent, blue, is the winner for month 13. We continue calculation for all 12 months and compute the average percentage—called red factor, blue factor, or green factor. Whichever is closest to 100 percent is the choice.

MESGRO Feature 3: Requirement of Only a Few Data Points

In the short-term model, MESGRO starts using the first two data points. To establish that MESGRO is able to track the structure of a particular data series, we make three forecasts—working with as few as five data points.

The long-run MESGRO uses half the given data points. With 12 months of data, the first half gives six data points to forecast months 7 to 12.

Table 9.2
Very Close Fit Very Rapidly

Observed	Expected	Chi-Squared
1. 1,800		
2. 2,100		
3. 2,600	2,097	120.65
4. 3,050	2,593	80.35
5. 3,100	3,041	1.14
6. 3,050	3,050	0.00

Stage-of-Growth G_2=Rapid Growth

With the addition of 1 Data-Point,

1 Change in Growth Stage
2 Change in Recent-Remote Split

MESGRO Feature 4: Adaptive Adjustment to Violent Fluctuations

In the next section, MESGRO results, we will demonstrate an accurate forecast one month after actual data jumped nearly 45 percent (shown in fig. 9.1).

MESGRO Feature 5: Self-Validation

Both short-and long-term MESGRO approaches establish how closely data points are forecast. Why should one trust MESGRO forecasts for months 25, 26, . . . 48? Look at the accuracy of actuals forecast in months 13 to 24, based on months one to 12.

MISSION APPLICATION 8: MESGRO RESULT 1—
WEAPONS SYSTEM COSTS IN CONTINUING PHASE

The real-life data presented in figure 9.1 relate to a segment of a weapon system; hence the application is a mission application. The question is: Given the data for 24 consecutive time periods, what should the management plan be for time period 25?

The fit in figure 9.2 (dotted line) hits 20 out of 22 points, lending considerable credibility to the $5.7-million forecast for month 25.

Table 9.3a
Dramatic Change in Growth Stage

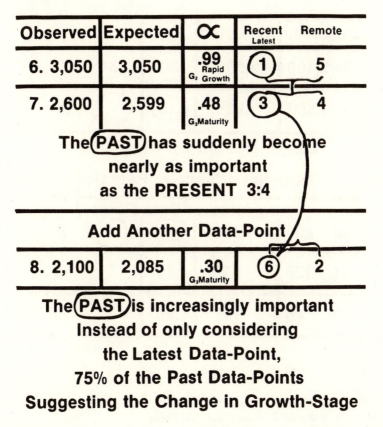

Observed	Expected	α	Recent Latest	Remote
6. 3,050	3,050	.99 Rapid G_2 Growth	①	5
7. 2,600	2,599	.48 G_3Maturity	③	4

The (PAST) has suddenly become
nearly as important
as the PRESENT 3:4

Add Another Data-Point

8. 2,100	2,085	.30 G_3Maturity	⑥	2

The (PAST) is increasingly important
Instead of only considering
the Latest Data-Point,
75% of the Past Data-Points
Suggesting the Change in Growth-Stage

Table 9.1 presents actual data and the MESGRO forecast. With the exception of the first forecast (always discarded as the first attempt by the program to orient itself), there is only one forecast significantly different from the actual. That point is the one representing a 45 percent jump in actual data for one month. MESGRO, however, adapted quickly to the violent jump, and came in on the money in the next period.

MARKET APPLICATION 9: MESGRO RESULT 2—
CHEMICAL SALES GROWTH STAGE WITH EVERY NEW
DATA POINT

The acronym MESGRO includes "growth." MESGRO not only provides a forecast—the content—but also provides the stage of growth of the life cycle of the product/program—the context.

Everything that is born, dies; and before it dies it declines. Decline comes

Table 9.3b
Dramatic Change in Growth Stage

Observed	Expected	∝	Recent	Remote
8 2,100	2,085	.30 G₃ Maturity	6	2
9 1,500	1,886	(.10) G₃	(7)	2
Larger No. of Past Data-Points					
Less Importance to Past Data			.48 .30 .10	
Add Another Data-Point					
10 800	1,510	(.99) G₄ Decline	(1)	9
11 125	816	.99 G₄	1	10
12 40	146	.99 G₄	1	11
13	?			

after maturity, which is reached after rapid growth. Prior to rapid growth is infancy, which comes after gestation and birth.

Products and programs are also subject to this seven-stage life cycle. Decision makers need to know at which stage their product or program is. At rapid growth one prepares for accelerated sales/costs. At maturation one prepares for decelerated sales/costs.

Since MESGRO deals with products/programs already in existence, three states—conception, birth, and death—do not apply. As shown in figure 9.3, four stages are relevant: infancy (G1), rapid growth (G2), maturation (G3), and decline (G4).

Real-life data do not behave ideally, progressing from G1 to G2, and G2 to G3, which makes specification of growth stage with each new data point as important as it is difficult. It is important, because of the guideline it provides. It is difficult, because unlike the smooth curve in figure 9.3, the real data points shoot up and down, alternating between, say, the rapid growth and the infancy stages.

To help interpret growth stages, MESGRO shows the number of data points

Fig. 9.4
Continuing Phase—MESGRO Forecast—Sales Monthly

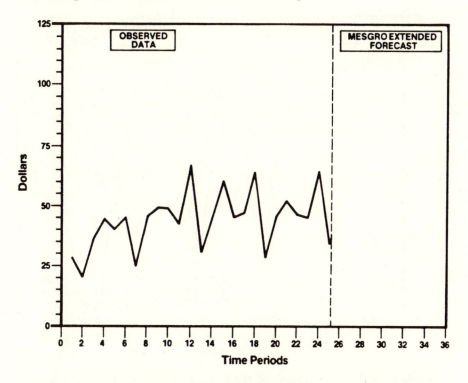

in recent and remote segments that provide the best fit to the data. Further, changes in the split between recent and remote segments provide important clues.

Consider data on the sale of a chemical product. First-year sales are 1,800,000 units, the second year, 2,100,000 units. Omitting the thousands, first-year sales reach 1800, the second year 2100. Sales increase to 2600 in the third year, 3050 in the fourth, 3100 in the fifth. Now sales decrease to 3050 in the sixth year, 2600 in the seventh, 2100 in the eight, 1500 in the ninth, 800 in the tenth, and further to 125 in the eleventh and to 40 in the twelfth.

We find from table 9.2 that the expected values provided by MESGRO zero in dramatically on the actual by the third forecast. The first forecast is an initialization, and thus it is not counted in the accuracy of the fit. The fit index, which is best when its value is zero, rapidly decreases to 80.35 in the second forecast, and to 1.14 in the third forecast. The stage of growth, as shown in table 9.3, is rapid growth.

When new data point number 8 is added to table 9.3, there is a dramatic shift in both the recent and remote split, and in growth stage. G2, rapid growth, is followed by G3, maturity. Turning to the split of past data points, we find at point 6 recent comprised only one data point and remote five points. However,

Fig. 9.5
Continuing Phase—MESGRO Forecast—Sales Monthly

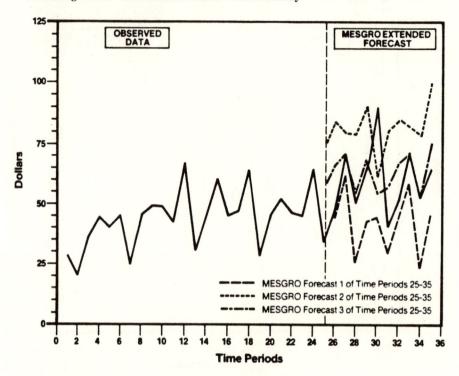

at data point 7, recent comprised three points instead of one. The past has suddenly become nearly as important as the present.

When data point 8 is added in table 9.3, recent comprised six data points, instead of three. The past is much more important than for data point 7. This increase in number of points in the recent category suggests a change in the growth stage. At data point 6 it was rapid growth, but maturity at points 7, 8, and 9, changing to rapid decline for points 10, 11, and 12.

Identification of growth stage with every new data point is invaluable. The user is alerted to changes in the offing, as from rapid growth to maturity, implying one should plan to cut production because demand is easing. On the other hand, the user could decide to increase advertisement of the product, and/or increase trade discounts making the product more competitive, and perhaps reverse the change in growth stage.

MARKET APPLICATION 10: MESGRO RESULT 3—
PRODUCT SALES IN CONTINUING PHASE

We will discuss four data sets relating to four important business factors— sales, prices, interest, and cost.

Table 9.4
Extended Forecast 2 and Forecast 3 of Cumulative Dollar Sales Made in Month 24 of Months 25–35, and Actuals as Percent of Forecast 2 and Forecast 3

Data-point	ACTUAL Cumulative	FORECAST 2 Cumulative	Actual/ Fcst. 2	FORECAST 3 Cumulative	Actual/ Fcst. 3
25	1112.4	1151.6	96.6%	1135.2	98.0%
26	1159.0	1236.0	93.8%	1201.2	96.5%
27	1229.9	1315.9	93.5%	1272.6	96.6%
28	1280.1	1394.9	91.8%	1327.2	96.5%
29	1345.2	1485.3	90.6%	1395.6	96.4%
30	1435.1	1547.1	92.8%	1449.7	99.0%
31	1475.8	1627.8	90.7%	1506.7	97.9%
32	1527.5	1713.4	89.1%	1573.9	97.1%
33	1599.3	1795.6	89.1%	1645.5	97.2%
34	1651.8	1874.1	88.1%	1698.3	97.3%
35	1716.8	1974.5	86.9%	1774.2	96.8%
	Average	Percent	91.2%		97.2%

Market forecasts are ubiquitous in sales departments. Given highly irregular data for 24 consecutive time periods as shown in Figure 9.4, what will monthly sales be for the next 12 time periods?

Time period 1 in Figure 9.4 records sales of $30 million. Sales did not begin in time period 1, but long before. Management simply chose the beginning of the period in which they were interested. Since the observed data relate to a continuing series, we refer to it as "continuing phase."

We provide three forecasts—red, blue, and green—so named to avoid connotations of preference implicit in 1, 2, and 3. Which is the best forecast for the given data? We divide the actual by red, blue, and green forecast to arrive at the respective factors, the closest to 100 percent being the best fit.

Figure 9.5 presents three forecasts; the green forecast (dot-dash line in center) is closest to the solid (yellow) line of actuals. Marketing management asked us to ignore the spike in the 30th period caused by year-end sales, which also accounted for the valley the next month. In other words, given erratic data, the green forecast is closest to the actual.

In the case of highly erratic data, it is better to work with cumulative figures. Individual fluctuations are thereby smoothed out. Figure 9.5 bears this out. The closeness of the green cumulative forecast (dot-dash line in center) to the solid (yellow) actuals is readily apparent. The average green factor (forecast 3) is 97.20 percent as seen in table 9.4

Fig. 9.6
Continuing Phase—MESGRO Extended Forecasts—Mortgage Insurance
Applications—Monthly

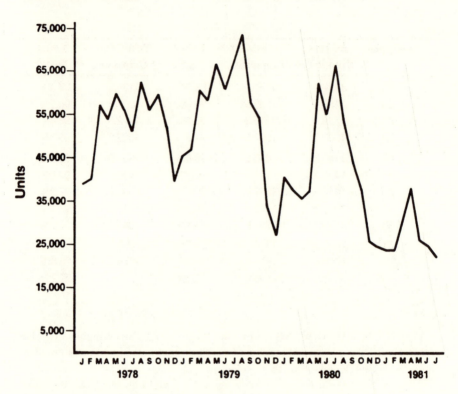

MARKET APPLICATION 11: MESGRO RESULT 4—PRIME
RATES IN CONTINUING PHASE

Interest rates are pervasive in their influence on business. How accurately interest rates can be forecast is a vital concern of top management.

The U.S. Department of Housing and Urban Development insures mortgages individuals take out when they build or buy a home. Since the government must commit itself to make good defaults on mortgages, which are based primarily on interest rates, the accuracy of a forecast of mortgage insurance applications depends on the accuracy of the prime rate forecast.

Figure 9.6 shows the number of mortgage insurance applications rising from 38,000 units to 75,000 units, and precipitiously dropping from 75,000 units to 25,000 units in three months when the prime rate hit its highest level in U.S. history. The question is: How should the number of mortgage insurance applications be forecast?

Figure 9.6 shows the number of mortgage insurance applications received by

Table 9.5
Red, Blue, and Green Factors Yielding Actual Data Points Observed

FORECAST PERIOD	RED FACTOR	BLUE FACTOR	GREEN FACTOR
25.00	102.30	100.85	101.77
26.00	105.67	100.33	103.67
27.00	108.28	99.85	105.06
28.00	110.62	99.10	106.14
29.00	115.33	100.31	109.39
30.00	118.69	101.09	111.64
31.00	123.08	101.92	114.46
32.00	125.09	102.49	115.82
33.00	126.21	102.42	116.39
34.00	126.33	102.72	116.60
35.00	126.74	102.95	116.93
36.00	127.72	103.02	117.50
37.00	128.37	102.19	117.45
38.00	130.06	101.91	118.21
39.00	131.19	101.62	118.66
40.00	132.71	101.49	119.38
41.00	133.77	100.93	119.64
42.00	134.21	99.82	119.30
43.00	134.76	99.14	119.22
44.00	0.00	0.00	0.00
45.00	0.00	0.00	0.00
46.00	0.00	0.00	0.00
47.00	0.00	0.00	0.00
48.00	0.00	0.00	0.00
34.00	123.67	101.29	114.49

the U.S. Department of Housing dramatically declined after the prime rate hit its highest level in U.S. history. MESGRO used the first 24 months to forecast months 25 to 43 (table 9.5). The blue factor for the cumulative averaged 101.29 percent, remarkable when considering the unique prime rate peak reached during the period, and consequent erratic data.

MARKET APPLICATION 12: MESGRO RESULT 5—
BRAZILIAN FEIJAO PRICES IN COMMENCEMENT PHASE

The data in Figure 9.7 are from the Inter-American Development Bank, which lends to South American countries and corporations for long-term industrial and

Fig. 9.7

Continuing Phase—Prices Paid for Cloreto de Potassio and Prices Received for Feijao

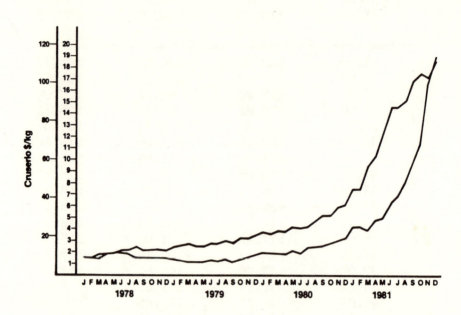

agricultural development. For this Brazilian agricultural loan the agricultural expert considered: prices paid by the farmer for potassium chlorate fertilizer (inside curve) and prices received by farmers for corn (outside curve). Both prices start at 1.5 Brazilian cruserio $/kilogram in January 1978. Data can be realistically considered to apply to the true start time (i.e., relate to the commencement phase).

When making long-term loans, the Inter-American Development Bank must forecast prices in the far future. Table 9.6 shows a forecast of prices received by the farmer for feijao—Brazilian corn—predicting cruserio dollar CR$112.54 for month 25. Why trust his figure? Notice that error is insignificant in the monthly price forecast. Cumulative deviations, or fit index, in the last column add up to 27 for the 24 points, more than half contributed by a single observation when observed data jumped from 69.3 to 99.7 in one month.

On what future price can the bank base its lending decisions? Table 9.7 shows that based only on 24 months of data, MESGRO forecasts the highest price will be CR$188 reached 20 months hence. It could go down to CR$114 at worst, but will probably be CR$172 32 months hence!

What will the farmer pay for potassium chlorate, his key fertilizer? The highest price, forecast at CR$31, will be reached 20 months hence when the price of

Table 9.6
Prices Received for Feijao—MESGRO Fit

No.of Data Points (T)	%Growth X(T) ---- X(1)	X(T) ------ X(T-1)	Gro- wth Stage	Best al- pha	Ex- pect- ed (T+1)	Ob- ser- ved (T+1)	Re- ce- nt T	Re- mo- te T	FIT INDEX Ind- ivi- dual	FIT INDEX Cum- ula- tive
2	111.4	111.4	G2	0.79	11.6	11.6	1	2	0.0	0.
3	108.9	97.8	G1	0.16	10.8	10.8	2	2	0.0	0.
4	101.6	93.3	G2	0.99	11.4	13.1	3	2	0.3	0.
5	123.6	121.9	G2	0.87	12.9	12.9	1	5	0.0	0.
6	121.2	98.0	G2	0.99	13.0	14.0	2	5	0.1	0.
7	131.9	108.9	G2	0.99	14.0	15.3	1	7	0.1	0.
8	143.9	109.1	G2	0.99	15.2	15.9	1	8	0.0	0.
9	149.7	104.1	G2	0.99	15.9	16.3	1	9	0.0	0.
10	154.0	102.8	G2	0.99	16.3	17.9	1	10	0.2	0.
11	168.9	109.7	G2	0.99	17.9	19.0	1	11	0.1	0.
12	179.1	106.0	G2	0.99	19.0	25.5	1	12	2.2	3.
13	239.7	133.9	G2	0.99	25.3	26.7	1	13	0.0	3.
14	250.9	104.7	G2	0.87	24.5	24.5	2	13	0.0	3.
15	230.4	91.8	G2	0.99	25.5	28.4	2	14	0.3	3.
16	267.0	115.9	G2	0.99	28.2	30.0	1	16	0.1	3.
17	282.1	105.6	G2	0.99	29.8	38.0	1	17	2.2	5.
18	357.8	126.8	G2	0.99	37.8	41.8	1	18	0.4	6.
19	394.0	110.1	G2	0.99	41.6	47.9	1	19	1.0	7.
20	451.4	114.6	G2	0.99	47.7	59.1	1	20	2.8	9.
21	556.8	123.3	G2	0.99	58.8	69.3	1	21	1.9	11.
22	652.9	117.3	G2	0.99	68.9	99.7	1	22	13.8	25.
23	939.0	143.8	G2	0.99	99.0	113.4	1	23	2.1	27.
AVG.	278.0	111.4	G2	0.93	Expected Next Value 112.54					

Table 9.7
Prices Received for Feijao—MESGRO Projection for 32 Months

I.APPROACHING THE ASYMPTOTE -22 Months Beyond observed Data

No. of Data Points	% Growth X(T) ----- X(1)	X(T) ----- X(T-1)	Expe- cted Value (T+1)
23	939.0	143.8	99.7
24	1225.0	130.5	130.1
25	1321.2	107.8	140.3
26	1426.6	108.0	151.5
27	1484.0	104.0	157.6
28	1520.7	102.4	161.4
29	1595.9	105.0	169.5
30	1610.9	100.9	171.1
31	1647.6	102.3	175.0
32	1627.0	98.8	172.8
33	1638.2	100.7	174.0
34	1698.9	103.7	180.4
35	1709.0	100.6	181.5
36	1724.0	100.9	183.1
37	1728.2	100.2	183.5
38	1734.1	100.3	184.2
39	1746.0	100.7	185.4
40	1756.8	100.6	186.6
41	1754.3	99.8	186.3
42	1776.4	101.3	188.7
43	1769.0	99.6	187.9
44	1766.6	99.9	187.6

Table 9.7 (*Continued*)

II. FORCED STEEP DECLINE -12 MONTHS BEYOND THE ASYMPTOTE

No. of Data Points	%Growth X(T) ---- X(1)	X(T) --- X(T-1)	Exp- ected Value (T+1)
45	1766.6	100.0	187.6
46	1766.6	100.0	187.6
47	1766.6	100.0	187.6
48	1480.5	83.8	157.2
49	1384.4	93.5	147.0
50	1279.0	92.4	135.8
51	1221.6	95.5	129.7
52	1185.4	97.0	125.9
53	1109.7	93.6	117.9
54	1094.6	98.6	116.3
55	1058.0	96.7	112.4
56	1078.5	101.9	114.5

the corn will be CR$188. Lowest price for fertilizer could be as low as CR$21, but will probably be CR$27 in month 56, 32 months beyond the last point.

MARKET APPLICATION 13: MESGRO RESULT 6—R&D COSTS IN CONCLUDING PHASE

In hi-tech business, interest and exchange rates are external factors of enormous significance. Investment in R&D—how much and for how long—is a significant internal factor. Costs can mount with no end in sight.

Figure 9.8 shows R&D costs for a second-generation product system. Originally expected to last 24 months, development was extended to 30, 36, 40, and 48 months successively. At the time MESGRO was applied, total actual costs stood at $34 million. The project manager wanted to know the cost over the next 12 months so that it could be controlled.

His question had to be rephrased. The appropriate question is: What should be the cost in succeeding months for the program to end at a given data point?

Table 9.7 (*Continued*)

III. FORCED SLOWER DECLINE -12 MONTHS BEYOND ASYMPTOTE

No. of Data Points	%Growth $\frac{X(T)}{X(1)}$	$\frac{X(T)}{X(T-1)}$	Expected Value (T+1)
45	1755.4	162.8	186.4
46	1694.7	96.5	180.0
47	1684.6	99.4	178.9
48	1669.6	99.1	177.3
49	1665.3	99.7	176.9
50	1659.5	99.6	176.2
51	1647.6	99.3	175.0
52	1636.8	99.3	173.8
53	1639.3	100.1	174.1
54	1617.2	98.7	171.8
55	1624.6	100.5	172.5
56	1627.0	100.2	172.8

The program manager asked if the program could be concluded in 84 months. Since this provided a termination point, the data series is in the concluding phase.

Designating the end-point to have zero cost, MESGRO seeks out alternates, forcing the cost curve to zero. Computationally, two successive negative quantities can fulfill the requirement. In table 9.8, only the blue forecast fulfills that condition. So we tell the program manager: If you want to finish by month 84, it will probably cost close to $46 million. High ranges are between $53 and $57 million (tab. 9.9).

MESGRO METHODOLOGY—SHORT- AND LONG-TERM

In both short and long term, MESGRO avoids imposing a model upon the data. Instead, it discovers the data's structure with each new point, determining the best way to split past data, and how best to weight them. When actual data are available, forecasts are corrected to closely track the actual—even when the actual data move violently up and down.

In the long term, instead of microsegments, macrosegments are selected to

Fig. 9.8
Concluding Phase—MESGRO Extended Forecasts—ACWP Monthly

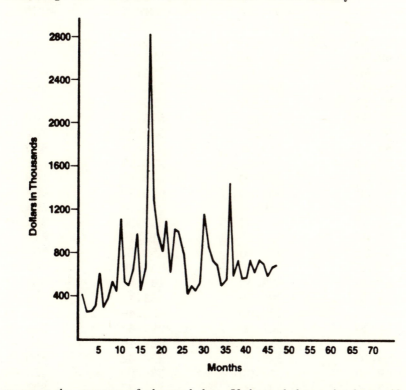

represent the structure of observed data. If the end data point is specified, MESGRO determines the best way to meet that specification, and gives two realistic ranges for the actual value that may be reached by cost/sales data.

In the short term, with the addition of every new data point, sales/cost, growth stage is determined. It tells the manager if he should gear up for increased production, level off, or decrease production ahead of time.

MESGRO's accuracy makes it suitable for control purposes. The difference between planned and actual is pinpointed by particular segments of sales/costs which are major contributors to the difference. Further, each difference is given a control factor by which the difference can be realistically controlled. A program manager can thus specify the specific results each submanager needs to achieve in the next period.

We developed basic MESGRO by discussing real-life examples. In the commencement phase, when sales/costs start from zero, our example was the forecast of ACWP (Actual Cost of Work Performed) values.

In the continuing phase, when sales (costs) continue unless otherwise indicated, two examples were used. The first involved the cost of a program whose first data point was $3,241,000 and 24th point was $5,869,000. The second

Table 9.8
MESGRO Plots of Forecast 1 (Red), Forecast 2 (Blue), and Forecast 3 (Green)

FORECAST PERIOD	RED MONTHLY	BLUE MONTHLY	GREEN MONTHLY
47.00	0.00	0.00	0.00
48.00	650.00	806.17	704.85
49.00	611.00	754.43	661.38
50.00	690.00	616.39	664.15
51.00	616.00	756.88	665.48
52.00	781.00	535.37	694.73
53.00	787.00	542.94	701.28
54.00	615.00	630.04	620.28
55.00	769.00	290.69	601.00
56.00	−89.00	644.15	168.51
57.00	698.00	612.13	667.84
58.00	846.00	335.14	666.57
59.00	669.00	398.30	573.92
60.00	621.00	614.19	618.61
61.00	483.00	552.87	507.54
62.00	195.00	−535.78	−61.68
63.00	828.00	197.51	606.55
64.00	889.00	363.41	704.40
65.00	856.00	430.49	706.55
66.00	941.00	299.68	715.75
67.00	556.00	569.76	560.83
68.00	329.00	330.42	329.50
69.00	303.00	336.20	314.66
70.00	731.00	438.37	628.22
71.00	257.00	386.62	302.53
72.00	536.00	248.59	435.05
73.00	361.00	389.08	370.86
74.00	74.00	167.57	106.87
75.00	−1461.00	175.14	−886.33
76.00	682.00	262.24	534.57
77.00	896.00	−77.11	554.21
78.00	387.00	276.34	348.13
79.00	727.00	244.32	557.47
80.00	847.00	−32.66	538.03
81.00	830.00	30.49	549.19
82.00	229.00	246.39	235.11
83.00	924.00	185.07	664.46
84.00	827.00	−903.59	219.16
85.00	968.00	−170.29	568.20
86.00	1062.00	−4.39	687.45

—NOTES—

Table 9.9
MESGRO Cumulative Forecast 1 (Red), Cumulative Forecast 2 (Blue), and Cumulative Forecast 3 (Green)

FORECAST PERIOD	RED CUMULATIVE	BLUE CUMULATIVE	GREEN CUMULATIVE
47.00	34085.00	34085.00	34085.00
48.00	34735.00	34891.17	34789.85
49.00	35346.00	35645.60	35451.23
50.00	36036.00	36261.99	36115.38
51.00	36652.00	37018.87	36780.86
52.00	37433.00	37554.25	37475.59
53.00	38220.00	38097.19	38176.87
54.00	38835.00	38727.23	38797.15
55.00	39604.00	39017.92	39398.15
56.00	39515.00	39662.07	39566.66
57.00	40213.00	40274.20	40234.49
58.00	41059.00	40609.34	40901.06
59.00	41728.00	41007.63	41474.98
60.00	42349.00	41621.82	42093.59
61.00	42832.00	42174.69	42601.13
62.00	43027.00	41638.91	42539.46
63.00	43855.00	41836.43	43146.01
64.00	44744.00	42199.84	43850.41
65.00	45600.00	42630.32	44556.95
66.00	46541.00	42930.00	45272.70
67.00	47097.00	43499.76	45833.53
68.00	47426.00	43830.19	46163.03
69.00	47729.00	44166.39	46477.69
70.00	48460.00	44604.76	47105.91
71.00	48717.00	44991.38	47408.44
72.00	49253.00	45239.97	47843.49
73.00	49614.00	45629.05	48214.36
74.00	49688.00	45796.62	48321.22
75.00	48227.00	45971.76	47434.89
76.00	48909.00	46234.00	47969.45
77.00	49805.00	46156.88	48523.66
78.00	50192.00	46433.23	48871.80
79.00	50919.00	46677.55	49429.27
80.00	51766.00	46644.89	49967.30
81.00	52596.00	46675.38	50516.49
82.00	52825.00	46921.77	50751.59
83.00	53749.00	47106.84	51416.06
84.00	54576.00	46203.25	51635.22
85.00	55544.00	46032.97	52203.41
86.00	**56606.00**	**46028.587**	**52890.86**

— NOTES —

Table 9.10
Commencement Phase and Continuing Phase

Defense Products Sales — Monthly
Sales Cumulative — Average (Actual/Fcst. 3) = 97.20%

Mortgage Insurance Applications — Monthly
Applications Cumulative — Average (Actual/Fcst. 2) = 101.29%

Beta Index — Monthly
Index Cumulative — Average (Actual/Fcst. 2) = 100.44%

Church Collections — Weekly
Collections Cumulative — Average (Actual/Fcst. 2) = 98.88%

Capital Equipment Index — Monthly
Equipment Index Cumulative — Average (Actual/Fcst.1) = 100.58%

Index of Materials and Components for Manufacturing — Monthly
Materials Index Cumulative — Average (Actual/Fcst. 1) = 100.18%

Prices Paid for Cloreto de Potassium — Monthly
Prices MONTHLY — 95.5% Forecasts 100.0% Accurate

Prices Received for Feijão — Monthly
Prices MONTHLY — 100% Forecasts 100% Accurate

example was sales of a chemical product group whose first data point was 1,800,000 units and 12th point was 40. Based on the difference between the planned and actual in the 25th period, specific controllable cost excesses in each contributing component can be identified.

In the concluding phase, MESGRO specified month-by-month ranges of figures within which program costs should fall in order for the program to end as desired.

MESGRO fits the model to the data, instead of data to the model, so that managers can control outcome by design, instead of by default, based on the high accuracy achieved as illustrated in table 9.10. The MESGRO methodology is presented in table 9.11.

CONCLUDING OBSERVATIONS

In chapter 8, we noted the need for dependable forecasts of technology to guide the decision to push for further improvements in the properties of the present product, or to try an altogether different approach to developing a new product. When larger and larger inputs yield smaller and smaller improvements,

Table 9.11
MESGRO Methodology

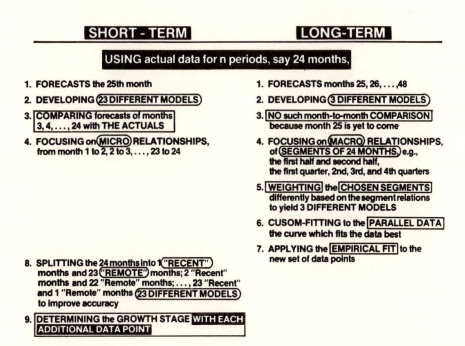

SHORT - TERM	LONG-TERM
USING actual data for n periods, say 24 months,	
1. FORECASTS the 25th month	1. FORECASTS months 25, 26, . . . ,48
2. DEVELOPING 23 DIFFERENT MODELS	2. DEVELOPING 3 DIFFERENT MODELS
3. COMPARING forecasts of months 3, 4, . . . , 24 with THE ACTUALS	3. NO such month-to-month COMPARISON because month 25 is yet to come
4. FOCUSING on MICRO RELATIONSHIPS, from month 1 to 2, 2 to 3, . . . , 23 to 24	4. FOCUSING on MACRO RELATIONSHIPS, of SEGMENTS OF 24 MONTHS, e.g., the first half and second half, the first quarter, 2nd, 3rd, and 4th quarters
	5. WEIGHTING the CHOSEN SEGMENTS differently based on the segment relations to yield 3 DIFFERENT MODELS
	6. CUSOM-FITTING to the PARALLEL DATA the curve which fits the data best
	7. APPLYING the EMPIRICAL FIT to the new set of data points
8. SPLITTING the 24 months into 1 "RECENT" months and 23 "REMOTE" months; 2 "Recent" months and 22 "Remote" months; . . . , 23 "Recent" and 1 "Remote" months 23 DIFFERENT MODELS to improve accuracy	
9. DETERMINING the GROWTH STAGE WITH EACH ADDITIONAL DATA POINT	

it suggests changing the tack. Similarly, if additional marketing (territory) effort yields smaller increase in market share, it suggests a change in tactics.

Several desirable criteria of forecasts were identified, such as high accuracy with few data points. A new computer-based numerical forecasting method, MESGRO, fills these criteria well in applications to 45 real-life instances of data. Six different applications were presented, including R&D costs, chemical sales growth, and prime rates. The technology manager can use MESGRO to develop dependable forecasts of both technology and territory.

Part IV

Bargaining
between Inventions
and Innovations

CONCOL
Bargaining:
Missions Context
of Markets

OVERVIEW: Charged with the survival of the country or the corporation, the technology manager has to resolve the conflicts between inventions and innovation as an ongoing process. How to recognize, identify, and resolve the conflicts is the aim of CONCOL process which requires areas of bargaining, measures of outcome, and changes by bargaining.

These three elements are developed in a discussion of the Cuban missile crisis. To explore areas of negotiation between Kennedy and Khrushchev, the need index is developed empirically. A need is a mandatory requirement, the nonfulfillment of which will significantly impair the basic mission and/or injure the basic capabilities of the entity. A want is a nonmandatory requirement. The exponents of the need index can be negative, zero, or positive; N-positive means the least negotiable position.

The CONCOL process aims to shift the party from an N-positive to an N-zero position. In the new position, the parties try to change the values to their advantage. Initial and eventual values of the outcome indicate how the bargaining is progressing.

Not only in political and military encounters, but also in business pursuits, countries play a key role. A dramatic instance of the conflict between corporate markets and national missions is provided by the 1987 transfer of U.S. technology by Japan and Norway to the Soviet Union which permits them to make their submarines quiet enough to avoid U.S. detection.

We find that both Japan and the United States want U.S. technology transfer to take place. However, when U.S. computerized milling machinery is exported by Japan to the Soviet Union, the economic transaction moves into the military realm. Economic penalties already imposed by the United States include the exclusion of offending Toshiba from the U.S. market for two years. A sore point in the U.S.-Japanese relationship is Japan's mounting trade surplus with the United States and the continued inaccessibility of Japanese markets to U.S. exports.

An articulate spokesman for Japan is Kenichi Ohmae, Managing Director of McKinsey & Co. in Tokyo. He proposes a common market between the two countries. The intriguing idea would take the edge off the trade surplus and market access. However, absent a strong government push, it is N-negative.

The country (missions) context of exports (markets) is brought into sharp relief by CONCOL. It provides an analytical framework to realistically represent the multifold issues and instances of conflict both within and between countries and corporations.

AT STAKE: SURVIVAL ON TWO FRONTS

The technology manager is charged with survival. He is judged by a single criterion: survival of the country or the corporation. Missions, primarily military, determine if a country survives or not; markets, domestic and foreign, determine if a corporation survives or not.

INTERACTION BETWEEN MISSIONS AND MARKETS

Without economic strength, missions cannot succeed. Without profits, corporations cannot survive. Without markets, profits cannot survive. Therefore, missions cannot succeed without markets.

To survive, the country manages not only missions, but also markets. Country policies directly affect the corporations' pursuit of markets, domestic and foreign, making conflicts inevitable. How to recognize, identify, and resolve the conflicts is the aim of CONCOL.

THE CONCOL PROCESS

In CONCOL, the process can be the product. The three critical elements of the CONCOL process are: (1) areas of bargaining (*why*?); (2) measures of outcome (*what*?); and (3) changes by bargaining (*how*?).

We will develop the three elements with respect to a historic example. Motivation for the CONCOL process is provided by a contemporary mission application in which we find a technology transfer between allies becoming a simultaneous technology transfer between allies and adversary. Given the dramatically undesirable CONCOL, we will then proceed to develop the three elements of the CONCOL process essential to diffusing the conflict, if not resolving it.

MISSION APPLICATION 9: ALLIES' TRANSFER OF U.S. TECHNOLOGY TO ADVERSARY—U.S. COMPUTERIZED MILLING MACHINERY TRANSFERRED TO THE SOVIET UNION BY JAPAN AND NORWAY

A dramatic instance of the conflict between corporate markets and national missions is provided by the 1987 transfer of U.S. technology by Japan and

Norway to the Soviet Union, which permits them to make their submarines quiet enough to avoid U.S. detection.

Foreign Market for U.S. Technology

The export of computerized milling machinery by the U.S. firm to Japan is a laudable effort. It provides earnings and profit to the exporter, and valuable products and services to the Japanese importer.

Foreign Market for Japanese Exports

Export of U.S. computerized milling machinery imported by Japan is a laudable effort. It provides earnings and profit to the Japanese exporter, and valuable products and services to the importer.

Private Sector Versus Public Sector on Technology Transfer

What makes a laudable effort by the private sector in the United States and Japan a not laudable effort is the conflict between markets and missions.

U.S. computerized milling machinery used by Japanese firm(s) for milling furthers the market interests of both countries. However, U.S. computerized milling machinery used by the Soviets to defeat the mission interests of the United States brings the Japanese private sector into direct conflict with the U.S. public sector.

Market and Mission CONCOL

The conflict can be presented as a CONCOL:

> U.S. private sector With Japanese private sector in U.S. technology transfer

> Japanese private sector With the U.S. private sector in U.S.-Japanese technology transfer

However, when Japan transfers the transferred technology which is used to defeat U.S. mission, there is direct conflict.

> Japanese private sector With the Soviet Union Against the U.S. public sector in Japan-Soviet technology transfer

Thus Japan is with the United States, and simultaneously against the United States.

CONCOL Bargaining

When two parties do not see eye-to-eye on a given situation, how can the interests of both be met? They use bargaining. Bargaining is the process of offer and counteroffer of future outcome(s) in return for present association(s). The CONCOL process is CONCOL bargaining.

In the summer of 1987 it was known that a subsidiary of Toshiba and a state-owned Norwegian arms company, Kongsberg Vaapenfabrikk, sold to the Soviet Union the U.S. advanced technology of computerized milling machinery. Several "offers" and "counteroffers" could be identified:

1. On July 1 the U.S. Senate voted 95 to 2 to ban sales by Toshiba and Kongsberg for two-five years.
2. The ban could also apply to any diversions listed in the Norwegian police reports after January 1, 1980. In October 1987, the Norwegian police report found that for ten years Kongsberg has been illegally diverting hi-tech to the Soviet Union, in collusion with firms in France, Italy, and West Germany, and as with Toshiba.
3. The chairman of Toshiba resigned although the illegal diversion was carried out by a subsidiary of Toshiba.
4. Japan and Norway promised to improve their export controls.

Clearly, this list of "offer" and "counteroffer" is just a beginning. The underlying issues are far-reaching. To resolve the conflict, or diffuse it, we need to develop a bargaining framework with reference to a historical mission situation.

MISSION APPLICATION 10: KENNEDY–KHRUSHCHEV CONCOL BARGAINING ON CUBA (N-Positive)

Consider the Cuban missile crisis. The confrontation and the compromise of the crisis can be understood in CONCOL terms.

CONCOL Bargaining Element 1: Areas of Bargaining (Why?)

It is interesting to note that Khrushchev used terminology about Kennedy at the Vienna talks, their first face-to-face encounter, which emphasized their simultaneously opposite roles:

I'd like to say a few words about the way Kennedy conducted his side of the Vienna talks. We were sitting in a room with only our interpreters, Rusk and Gromyko. . . . John Kennedy and I met man to man, as the two principal representatives of our countries. He felt perfectly confident to answer questions and make points on his own. This was to his credit, and he rose in my estimation at once. *He was, so to speak, both my partner and my adversary*. Insofar as we held different positions, he was my *adversary*; but insofar as we were negotiating with each other and exchanging views, he was my *partner* whom I treated with great respect. [emphasis added][1]

We may paraphrase Khrushchev as follows:

Kennedy With Khrushchev on coexistence

Khrushchev Against Kennedy on status quo maintenance

Kennedy wanted to maintain *status quo* in the world. I was also in favor of the *status quo*, and still am, but we differed in our understanding of what this term meant. For us "maintaining the *status quo*" meant agreeing not to violate the borders that came into existence after World War II—and especially not to violate them by means of war. Kennedy, however, had in mind the inviolability of the borders *plus the enforced preservation of a country's internal social and political system.* In other words, he wanted countries with capitalist systems to remain capitalist, and he wanted us to agree to a guarantee to that effect.

This was absolutely unacceptable. At that time many people still lived under colonialism. Did he really expect us to help the colonialists continue their oppression of their colonies? [emphasis added][2]

Areas of Agreement and Disagreement

In the light of Khrushchev's amplification, we can sharpen the agreement, as well as disagreement, between Khrushchev and Kennedy. "Coexistence" refers to the United States and the Soviet Union pursuing their present courses. In other words, it is status quo as far as superpowers are concerned. However, when it comes to status quo in countries other than the United States and the Soviet Union, Kennedy wanted them to be left alone, while Khrushchev wanted to have the freedom to engage in "wars of liberation." Thus we could restate the CONCOL as:

Khrushchev With Kennedy on status quo of superpowers

Khrushchev Against Kennedy on status quo of nonsuperpowers

Within the framework of this CONCOL, negotiations are possible. Khrushchev could not affect the status quo in all the nonsuperpowers at the same time. Therefore, he would be necessarily limited to confining his actions to upsetting the status quo of some of the nonsuperpowers. If Kennedy had a special interest in some of these nonsuperpowers, Khrushchev could agree not to rock the boat in those countries for the time being. In return, Khrushchev could demand maintaining the profile he desired in the other nonsuperpower countries. Or, he could demand contributions to the maintenance of status quo of the superpowers themselves.

In the Khrushchev-Kennedy CONCOL, the status quo of the superpowers was considered inviolate. In other words, the economic and social, the political and military aspects of the profile of one superpower could not be affected by the other superpower. While it is fully recognized that each power tries to influence the other, the maintenance of status quo requires that no drastic change in the existing economic and social, political and military aspects be made. What area(s) of the nonsuperpower profile is negotiable?

Negotiable Areas and Nonnegotiable Areas

Changes in the current profile of some of the nonsuperpowers would be permissible, but not of some others. Therefore, the first measure is the number of nonsuperpower countries that could be affected. Even among those countries whose profile could be affected, changes in certain aspects of the country profile could be tolerated, but not changes in some other, such as the military aspects; changes in the political aspects could be tolerated, but not in the military aspects.

The bargaining between the CONCOL members becomes the give-and-take on the basis of the evaluation by each party of the significance of the projected changes. The projected changes are by no means certain; therefore, the evaluation has to be in terms of probabilities of outcomes. The question of credibility of the promises by the other members is crucial.

We could reconstruct the Khrushchev–Kennedy CONCOL in terms of negotiable and nonnegotiable areas:

NONNEGOTIABLE: Superpower Profile—economic and social; political and military aspects

                   Nonsuperpower profile—military aspects

NEGOTIABLE: Nonsuperpower profile—economic and social aspects

NONNEGOTIABLE: Nonsuperpower profile—political aspects

CONCOL Bargaining Element 2: Measures of Outcome (What?)

It is one thing to identify areas of bargaining; it is quite another to assess acceptable outcomes. For instance, what does it mean to say that the military aspects of nonsuperpowers are not negotiable? Does it mean that the country in question cannot receive weapon supplies from external sources? Does it mean that the country in question cannot have technical advisors from outside? Does it mean that the training abroad of the present and/or potential leaders of the country in question is unacceptable?

It is in the very nature of bargaining that the initial positions taken by the parties to the bargaining are subject to change. The change will take place in reasonably equitable a manner if whatever is given up by one side is approximately equal to whatever it gains.

What constitutes equitable measure to the other side? What does it consider important?

The Cuban missile crisis, in retrospect, is an example of miscalculation of the outcome by the two parties involved. According to the *Last Testament*, Khrushchev believed that the United States, unhappy over the Bay of Pigs, would seek to overthrow Castro by bringing in the military in support of "counter-revolutionary forces" in Cuba. Because of the five thousand-mile distance, the Soviet Union would not be able to assist Cuba in that eventuality. That concern was part of his philosophy of "wars of liberation" which would set countries free from the yoke of "colonialists." Therefore, as a "defensive measure," simply to protect Cuba from "U.S. aggression," Khrushchev introduced Soviet missiles into Cuba. From Khrushchev's point of view, the introduction of missiles into Cuba was simply to maintain the status quo in the economic and social aspects of a nonsuperpower—aspects which were clearly negotiable as we saw above. However, Kennedy saw it as something entirely different.

He had no plans to invade Cuba, or to support an indigenous movement to overthrow Castro. Having accepted full blame for the Bay of Pigs fiasco, he would not rush into another Bay of Pigs. Suddenly, he was faced with missiles pointed at the heartland of America. At a time when the accuracy of missiles was far from established, missiles located five thousand miles away in the Soviet Union and United States of America would be approximately equal in their effectiveness or ineffectiveness. But when U.S. missiles are five thousand miles away from their targets, and the Soviet missiles are only 90 miles away from their targets, that does indeed tip the scales of military advantage decisively in favor of the Soviet Union. Therefore, from Kennedy's point of view, the introduction of Soviet missiles into Cuba was not to maintain the status quo in the economic and social aspects of the nonsuperpowers, but instead, to dramatically change the status quo of the military aspects of the superpower profile, which, as we saw above, was nonnegotiable.

To measure the negotiability and nonnegotiability of the issues to each party, it is necessary to develop an index of imperativeness.

Index of Imperativeness

We start by making a distinction between "needs" and "wants." The need for transportation, for instance, is met by walking, taking the bus, taking the subway or driving an automobile. If the need is to be met by driving an automobile, strictly from the point of view of fulfilling the need for transportation, a vehicle as functional as the Volkswagen Beetle or as luxurious as the Lincoln Continental could do the job. While the "need" for personal transportation is met by either, or a number of alternatives in between, only one can meet the "want."

A need is a mandatory requirement, the nonfulfillment of which will significantly impair the basic mission and/or injure the basic capabilities of the entity. A want is a nonmandatory requirement, which does not have to be satisfied in order to fulfill the basic mission or maintain the capabilities of the entity.

It should be recognized that the "want" of an earlier day may well become the "need" of a later day. Further, the assertion by one party to a CONCOL that something is a "need" could well be a bargaining posture. To make an operational measure out of the "need"-"want" combinations, it is fitting that a ratio be developed incorporating the admissible combinations. Since the extremes—all need and no want, or all want and no need—would make the ratio of need/want indeterminate, we could use 1 percent instead of 0 percent. The extreme ratios would thus be:

all want and no need = 99% want and 1% need; (need/want) = 1%/99% = 1/99 = .001

all need and no want = 1% want and 99% need: (need/want) = 99%/1% = 99/1 = 99.0

We can call the ratio of need/want the need ratio, or the N-index. The N-index can range from 0.01 to 99.0, or approximately $1/10^2$ to 10^2. When need = want, the ratio is 1, or 10^0. Thus, the exponent of the N-index can be negative, zero, or positive, making the situations N-negative, N-zero, or N-positive.

We stated in the last section that the superpower profile was nonnegotiable: for both Kennedy and Khrushchev, the N-index was positive, the maintenance of superpower profile unchanged being an imperative "need," making the numerator of the need/want ratio definitely higher than the denominator, yielding an index larger than one, with a positive exponent. We also said that the military aspects of nonsuperpower profiles were also nonnegotiable. The two N-positive positions led to a direct encounter. We can present the initial positions of encounter as follows:

N-positive Khrushchev With N-positive Kennedy on superpower profile status quo

N-positive Khrushchev Against N-positive Kennedy on superpower profile alternation

N-positive Khrushchev With N-zero Kennedy on nonsuperpower economic and social profile alteration

N-positive Khrushchev Against N-positive Kennedy on nonsuperpower military profile alteration

CONCOL Bargaining Element 3: Changes by Bargaining (How?)

Accommodations would be easier on N-zero positions than on N-positive positions. Taking the statements of Khrushchev in the *Last Testament* at face value, the reason for his introducing the missiles into Cuba was purely to ensure that the Cuban experiment in democratic living would be permitted to be conducted without foreign intervention. In other words, he had no interest in the military aspects of the nonsuperpower profile. Khrushchev was N-zero on nonsuperpower military profile alteration, but N-positive on nonsuperpower economic and social profile alteration. At the same time, Kennedy considered the particular nonsuperpower military profile alteration to be quite significant. Therefore, Kennedy would be N-positive on nonsuperpower military profile alteration. We can present the situation as follows:

N-positive Khrushchev Against N-zero Kennedy on nonsuperpower economic and social profile alteration

N-zero Khrushchev With N-positive Kennedy on nonsuperpower military profile alteration

Kennedy interpreted Khrushchev's claim to nonsuperpower economic and social profile alteration to be in fact superpower military profile alteration. Both would agree on the issue of superpower military profile status quo; therefore, Kennedy's objective of the Cuban missile crisis negotiations was to persuade Khrushchev that superpower military profile was in fact altered; it had to be restored. At the same time, taking the *Last Testament* at face value, Khrushchev's objective was to persuade Kennedy that nonsuperpower economic and social profile was threatened; it had to be removed. We can characterize the purpose of the bargaining to be that of letting each side know what the other side was N-positive about:

N-positive Kennedy against N-zero Khrushchev on superpower military profile alteration

N-positive Khrushchev against N-zero Kennedy on nonsuperpower economic and social profile alteration

The CONCOL Solution

The solution to the Cuban missile crisis could be interpreted as the progress from N-positive positions to N-zero positions.

Since the United States did not intend to invade Cuba or support anti-Castro uprising from within, the United States was N-zero with respect to economic and social profile alteration of Cuba. Similarly, strictly on the basis of *Last Testament*, the Soviet Union was N-zero with respect to superpower military profile. Therefore, the withdrawal of Soviet missiles from Cuba on the U.S. assurance of nonintervention in Cuba would provide a solution in the N-zero zone of both the United States and the Soviet Union.

MISSION APPLICATION 9 (CONCLUDED): CONCOL BARGAINING ON U.S.-JAPANESE TECHNOLOGY TRANSFER BECOMING JAPANESE-SOVIET TECHNOLOGY TRANSFER

There has to be areas of mutual interest which the CONCOL parties want to protect. Without them, there will be no bargaining.

Areas of Bargaining (Why?)

Japan wants to import U.S. technology of computerized milling machinery; and the United States wants to export it to Japan. The economic transaction moves into the military realm when Japan transfers the technology to the Soviet Union which uses it to build submarines quiet enough to avoid U.S. detection.

As we saw in the Kennedy–Khrushchev CONCOL, superpower military profile is nonnegotiable. The illegal Japanese transfer of U.S. technology to the Soviet Union did alter the superpower military profile.

The United States keeps asking Japan to make the Japanese market accessible to the United States. And Japan keeps saying that they are doing so. However, Japan remains rather inaccessible to the U.S. exporter.

Measures of Outcome (What?)

Having identified trade and technological aspects of U.S.-Japanese relationship as negotiable aspects, and the U.S.-Soviet military aspects as nonnegotiable, what kinds of outcomes are acceptable?

Initial CONCOL Positions on Trade

We start with the initial CONCOL positions:

N-positive U.S. government With N-positive Japanese government on superpower military profile status quo

N-positive U.S. government Against N-zero Japanese business on Japanese transfer of U.S. hi-tech imports to the Soviet Union

However, the issue of illegal transfer of U.S. technology cannot be effectively considered without reference to U.S.-Japanese trade.

N-positive Japanese government With N-positive U.S. government on expansion of Japanese-U.S. trade

N-zero Japanese government Against N-positive Japanese business on U.S. access to Japanese markets

We have characterized as "N-zero" the Japanese government positions on U.S. access to Japanese markets. If it were "N-positive", the situation is confrontational, making an aim of CONCOL to be to change it from N-positive to N-zero.

However, the position of Japanese business with respect to U.S. entry into the domestic market appears to be N-positive. Tough words, and even a temporary tariff in 1987 on selected Japanese exports to the United States, have not opened up Japan to U.S. exports. Keeping their market closed to the United States suggests an N-positive situation.

We referred earlier to the 95–2 vote in the U.S. Senate on July 1, 1987 to ban imports from Toshiba and Kongsberg for two to five years. The ban could be extended to other companies and countries which are found to have illegally transferred U.S. technology since 1980.

The ban could reduce to zero the imports in 1987–1989 from Toshiba. The chairman of the board of Toshiba resigned, assuming responsibility for the illegal actions of a subsidiary of Toshiba.

One measure of outcome that Japan would like to see is the restoration of Toshiba imports into the United States, and an increase of the same. On the part of the United States, one measure of outcome would be zero transfer by Toshiba to the Soviet Union of U.S. hi-tech exports.

Initial CONCOL Positions on Currency Exchange

Another measure would be the U.S. trade deficit with Japan. An articulate Japanese viewpoint places the blame on the United States:

The United States is frustrated with its huge trade deficits. . . . Now the United States one-sidedly gives the reason for the imbalance: Japanese markets are closed to the Americans. So our government has to come up with a series of "action plans" to rework tariffs and other trade restrictions. Today, Japan has one of the most liberal trade practices in the world.[3]

Kenichi Ohmae, managing director of McKinsey & Co., goes on to say that Japan and the United States have formed "an unbelievably interlinked financial and trading relationship." His argument is well understood in CONCOL terms:

The United States needs to depart from its traditional style of hegemonical *leadership*; and Japan should graduate from its time-honored habit of excusing itself and *play a real leadership role*—commensurate with its economic influence. . . .

Japan and the United States, the two financial superpowers, need to sit down and work out the details of *financial detente* . . . .

Potential benefits of *forming a common market.* . . . The merits of America's issuing some securities pegged to the yen to signal its seriousness about *currency stabilization* [bringing down] Japan's hyperinflated *land prices.* [emphasis added][4]

The idea of a U.S.-Japanese common market is intriguing. At this stage, lacking strong governmental push, it cannot be considered to rank high in priorities, giving it an N-negative index.

Currency stabilization could be considered N-zero, while the reduction of Japanese land prices could be considered N-negative.

The issue of Japanese leadership, requiring consultations and coordinated action on interest rates, exchange rates, and soon, is a long-term issue of significance. Insofar as it has not been voiced at the governmental level, much less lobbied for, we have to leave it at the N-negative level.

The key issue from the U.S. point of view is:

N-positive Japanese business Against U.S. access to Japanese markets

Such a position could never work without the permission and encouragement of the Japanese government. What outcomes can be considered effective in moving the N-positive Japanese business to an N-zero position?

Currency stabilization coordination may provide the most direct and visible enhancement of Japanese leadership. Will the Japanese government move from an N-zero to N-positive position on behalf of U.S. access to Japanese markets?

A concrete measure of outcome could be the increase in the U.S. share of Japanese imports in hi-tech fields, such as telecommunications, in which the U.S. effort in 1987 to bid was the latest to be rebuffed. Protectionist voices in Congress become more strident with each such occurrence, as reflected in the trade bill.

Changes by Bargaining (How?)

We can identify two types of changes by bargaining: (1) Change in the index of imperativeness; and (2) change in the index.

Change of the Index

In the Kennedy–Khrushchev CONCOL, the process moved the parties from confrontational N-positive positions to compromising N-zero positions. Both agreed that superpower military profile was nonnegotiable. What Kennedy had to do was to convince Khrushchev that Soviet missiles in Cuba did in fact violate the superpower military profile. Khrushchev could assure Kennedy that Soviet missiles in Cuba were not to alter the military profile in favor of the Soviet Union.

Based only on *Last Testament*, the Soviet missiles were introduced to prevent the alteration of the political profile of a specific nonsuperpower, Cuba, which Khrushchev thought Kennedy was likely to do. Kennedy could give Khrushchev a guarantee that he had no such intentions, which changed N-positive Khrushchev into N-zero status. Since Khrushchev was not upsetting superpower profile, he could take back the Soviet missiles, moving N-positive Kennedy to an N-zero status.

The most difficult change is the change of the index of imperativeness, the N-index.

With respect to U.S. access to Japanese markets, a reverse change in status of the N-index is required. The N-zero Japanese government has to be moved to N-positive status.

Unlike in the United States, Japanese business enjoys a uniquely Japanese institution, "administrative guidance." For instance, the government forecasts the foreign demand for Japanese steel, and "suggests" how it could be met by the various Japanese manufacturers of steel. The "administrative guidance" guarantees the foreign market every month.

It was under the strong prodding of the government, particularly the Ministry of International Trade and Industry (MITI) that the recalcitrant Japanese corporations were persuaded to manufacture automobiles in the United States. The Japanese government became N-positive with respect to Japanese manufacture in the United States. Why?

In retrospect, we could argue that MITI became convinced that unless Japan manufactured automobiles in the United States, it would face a shrinking market; certainly a decreasing increase in the market. A similar message, such as the passage and enforcement of a trade bill which Japan would consider strongly protectionist, would be required to move the Japanese government from N-zero to N-positive status.

Changes in the Index

The change of the index from N-positive to N-zero or vice versa sets the direction of CONCOL bargaining; the change in the value of the index from 1 to 99 calibrates the magnitude of CONCOL outcome.

The N-negative situation is no need (represented by .01) and all want (represented by 99), giving a need/want ratio of .01, or 10 to minus 2, making the exponent negative.

N-zero represents (.50 need/.50 want) = 1.0, or 10^0.

N-positive represents (.99/.01) = 99, or 10^2.

The effort to move the Japanese government from N-zero to N-positive with respect to U.S. access to Japanese markets gives a range of 1 (N-zero) to 2 (N-positive). What is the turning point? We could use the range midpoint, 1.5, as the value to watch. When it is exceeded, say at 1.6, we can say that the direction is away from N-zero and toward N-positive.

The range midpoint thus provides an index of direction through magnitude. The change in the index from 1.5 to 1.6 signifies a change of the index from N-zero to N-positive.

CONCLUDING OBSERVATIONS

The corporate technology manager will find that his markets impinge upon and are impinged upon by national interests (missions). A dramatic instance of the conflict between corporate markets and national missions is provided by the 1987 transfer of U.S. technology by Japan and Norway to the Soviet Union which permits them to make their submarines quiet enough to avoid U.S. detection.

CONCOL provides a framework to represent the conflicting interests of U.S. and Japanese public and private sectors. Clearly, the public sector in Japan would want the U.S. public sector to continue to guarantee military protection. At the same time, Toshiba is a large Japanese corporation in whose continued prosperity the Japanese public sector has unquestioned interest.

On the part of the United States, the private sector wants to export computerized milling technology (and other technology) to Japan. However, the U.S. private sector would not want to be accessory to selling to the Soviets U.S. technology which gives the Soviet Union military advantage.

To develop the CONCOL process elements, we examined the Cuban missile crisis. The hardest part was to develop areas of bargaining, without which there can be no negotiation. Drawing upon Khrushchev's own version of what happened, and more importantly what he thought at that time, we were able to construct certain areas open to negotiation. We specified measures of outcome which delineated the initial and eventual outcomes desired. The changes by bargaining show the progress toward the eventual outcomes on both sides.

Applying the CONCOL process to the U.S.-Japanese technology transfer we were able to identify areas of bargaining in the economic arena—trade and technology. However, illegal transfer of U.S. technology to the Soviet Union was clearly nonnegotiable. Strict export controls by Japan and Norway on U.S. technology would be part of the eventual outcome of negotiations in the area.

The changes by bargaining would be measured in terms of the changes in the direction of the index, such as that from positive to zero. N-positive positions are the least negotiable, making the shift to N-zero positions a critical necessity. Once the direction is changed, changes in magnitude become important.

The CONCOL process provides an operational framework to represent opposing interests in several dimensions, whether within and between corporations, or between corporation and country(ies). It will be applied to technology and to territory in the final chapter: the R&D investment decision of a multinational (technology) and the multinational's sharing in overseas markets (territory) newly created by the NIC for products imbedding the technology transferred by the multinational.

with a new product which could not have been made without the technology transfer.

CONCOL offers an analytic framework to explicate the opposing interests in several areas within the same corporation, between corporations, between corporation(s) and country, and between countries, as well as varying combinations. It also provides a bargaining process to achieve mutually beneficial results.

CORPORATE R&D INVESTMENT STRATEGY

The McKinsey study of technology management by leading U.S. enterprises, discussed in chapter 3 says: "[I]n the 25 years between 1955 and 1980, *all of the leading electronics manufacturers* in the United States *ceased to be significant* competitors in solid-state electronics" (emphasis added).[1]

How can corporations invest in R&D so that they do not become extinct in their own fields? IBM is an excellent example. We turn to its strategy of technology growth by design.

MARKET APPLICATION 14: TECHNOLOGY CONCOL— "AT IBM CORPORATE RESEARCH . . . ALWAYS HAS TWO MAJOR PROJECTS IN PLACE FOR EACH TECHNOLOGY"

The trajectory of improvement of performance characteristics cannot continue forever; otherwise the same product could be made better and better forever and keep satisfying the market. How can the corporation prepare ahead for the inevitable decline and death of today's improving performance characteristics?

Linear Extension Versus Quantum Jump

We said in chapter 7 that the forecast of linear extensions of performance characteristics calls for continuities methods, while the forecast of quantum jumps calls for discontinuities methods. To know when to use which method, it is critical to know the limits.

Always . . . Two Major Projects

IBM prepares for the future by determining what the limits are, and forging ahead with the most promising radical alternative. In the words of IBM's chief scientist, Lewis Branscomb:

At IBM we have an explicit way to deal with this limit. Our corporate research organization identifies all the major technologies on which our business depends—electronic logic technology, for example—and always has two major projects in place for each technology. *One is* aimed at determining what *limits* nature sets *to the improvement of current mainstream technology.* For electronic logic, that would be silicon electronic-circuit technology

CONCOL Bargaining: Intranational R&D Investment, International Technology Transfer

OVERVIEW: The buck stops with the corporate technology manager. He has to choose between improvement and invention. It can be represented as a conflict between the alter ego opting for invention, and the anti-ego opting for invention.

Superconducting Josephson technology was IBM's alternative in 1983. The research on it was later cut. However, in 1987 IBM Laboratories announced the breakthrough in superconductors, a development which is sure to alter the R&D investment strategy.

From the technology CONCOL, we turn to a territory CONCOL. The vast majority of the mounting volume of inventions piled up each year by IBM and other multinationals goes unused because the top 5 percent or so would yield more than enough returns. The other 95 percent is locked up in corporate vaults to safeguard the market for the top 5 percent.

The newly industrializing countries (NICs) can never even hope to come anywhere near the R&D investment of the likes of IBM. Even if they had the money, they do not have the personnel or the tradition of research. Therefore, they have to look to the multinationals for technology. Some of them have earned nasty reputations for piracy. Clearly, on the matter of preserving the intellectual property rights of the multinationals, they and the NICs have opposing interests. But are there any areas of bargaining?

If the NICs were to develop new markets overseas for products imbedding specific technology transferred by the multinationals to the NICs, and if the latter would share part of the market revenue with the former, there could be an area of bargaining generated by mutuality of interests. The level of the technology transferred would not be top-line technology. But if the NICs are at level 15 on the technology scale, and if the multinationals were to transfer technology level 45, it would raise the NIC level 300 percent without a single dollar spent in risky R&D. The NIC gets to develop its own market of ever smaller dimensions. *The second* project is aimed at *the single most promising radical alternative*. For electronic logic that would be superconducting Josephson technology or perhaps gallium arsenide technology. Thus we try to have knowledge of where *technical limits* are—knowledge that is quantitatively expressed and based on actual research—in order to better understand the *limits of* our *business* possibilities. [emphasis added][2]

We may paraphrase Branscomb's two perennial projects as one on linear extension and another on quantum jumps. The inherent opposition between the two is clarified in CONCOL terms. The same organization is at odds with itself, which we have termed earlier as the opposition of alter ego and anti-ego, the former committed to long-run interests, and the latter to short-term interests.

IBM alter ego With quantum jumps in performance characteristics Against linear extensions

IBM anti-ego Against quantum jumps in performance characteristics With linear extensions

Areas of Bargaining (Why?)

While the protagonists of linear extensions and quantum jumps are each fiercely advocating resources for their respective efforts for better results for IBM, it is not an either-or proposition. It is not as though the quantum jumps will automatically displace the entire array of linear extensions. The "area of bargaining" between these two opposing interests within IBM is the rate of introduction of the respective technology. Obviously, the IBM market is satisfied with the current value of the performance characteristics. Let us say that IBM commands 65 percent of the world market in that product (process) with the current value of the performance characteristics.

In the next time period, say 6 months, linear extensions of the performance characteristics will retain say 30 percent of the world market. The market share goes down to 15 percent in months 7–12, and to 5 percent in months 13–18. The very purpose of the quantum jumps is to retain the original 65 percent share of the world market and if possible, to enhance it.

The area of bargaining between alter ego and and anti-ego can be identified as the world market share of the product retained. If linear extensions are able to hold the initial 65 percent, the retention is 100 percent. In our illustration, the retention by linear extensions is (30/65 =) 46 percent during months 1–6; 23 percent in months 7–12; and 8 percent in months 13–18. To offset this projected loss in retention, quantum jumps will have to penetrate the market with the new product.

Measures of Outcome (What?)

We can measure the CONCOL outcome in terms of the ratio of retention to penetration or R/P ratio. When linear extension retains 32.5 percent of the world market of the particular product, and quantum jumps penetrate the remaining 32.5 percent of the original share, the ratio (32.5/ 32.5 =) is 1.0. When the retention is higher, say 40 percent and the penetration captures the remaining 25 percent, the ratio is (40/25 =) 1.6. In the initial stages, linear extensions are likely to be more successful, because the market is familiar with the product, making the value of the R/P ratio higher than 1. As the new product incorporating the quantum jump in performance characteristics becomes more familiar, the ratio will become lower than 1.

DRAMATIC QUANTUM JUMPS IN SUPERCONDUCTIVITY TECHNOLOGY

Branscomb referred to "superconducting Josephson technology" as "the single most promising radical alternative." Since Branscomb made the statement in 1983, IBM cut its research on Josephson technology.

Linear Extension Replaced by Dramatic Quantum Jump in Technology

Events in 1986 far outstripped the 1983 outlook. In early fall of 1986, the discovery by Muller and Bednorz at the IBM Zurich Research Laboratory of high transition temperature superconductivity was confirmed. The progression of the superconducting transition temperature (T) for the first 75 years provides an example of what we call "linear extension" in the performance characteristics, when a series of dramatic quantum jumps occurred:

Fig. [11.1] shows the progression of the superconducting transition temperatures (T) from the discovery of the phenomenon in mercury by H. K. Onnes in 1911 until February 1987. One notices a more or less linear increase in maximal T until the 75th anniversary of the discovery. This led to the expectation of Ts near 30K in 1990. However, in the year of the anniversary this trend changed. By the beginning of 1987, Ts had risen to 48K for the original compound and its isomorphs. At the beginning of February 1987, the confirmed Ts were over 90K in a Ba-Y-Cu oxide formed by Chu and collaborators and nearly, but not simultaneously at Bellcore and the Academy in Beijing.[3]

The increase is Ts from 5 in 1911 to 25K in 1986 works out to an annual average increase of 0.2667K a year. But a jump of 15K occurred in 1986; and another jump of 50K in 1987. In other words, the linear extension of 0.2667K a year for 75 years was displaced dramatically by a 56-fold increase in 1986, followed by a 337-fold increase in 1987.

Fig. 11.1
Evolution of the Superconductor Transition Temperature Subsequent to the Discovery of the Phenomenon

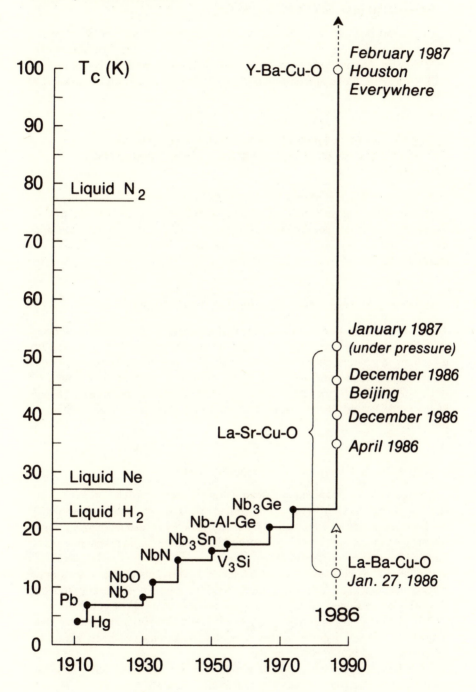

Applications of Accelerating Technology

Muller and Bednorz note that the new superconductors since 1986 are layer-like copper oxides. They are easy to fabricate, their Ts are very high, and above all, "they are of considerable technological importance, because in addition to the known applications summarized in [Fig. 11.2], they may allow cheap energy transfer."[4]

MARKET APPLICATION 16: TERRITORY CONCOL—U.S. TECHNOLOGY TRANSFER TO NEWLY INDUSTRIALIZING COUNTRIES (NICs)

As devastatingly demonstrated on Black Monday, October 19, 1987, the U.S. trade deficit and budget deficit are of utmost concern to the rest of the world. Unless the rest of the world finds it attractive to invest in the United States and the U.S. dollar, they will not continue to let the United States live beyond its means.

Motivation 1: Trade Drain and the U.S. Trade Deficit

The trade deficit is but a symptom of trade drain, which we have defined elsewhere as the international imbalance among the elements of the triad of invention, innovation, and instruction. Instead of treating the symptom, many argue that we should treat the cause by marrying U.S. strength in invention to Asian strength in enterprise through judicious technology transfer from the United States to the Pacific, increasing income from innovation as well as innovation for both.

Motivation 2: Mounting U.S. Corporate Assets

A large U.S. corporation, or a multinational, invests in R&D funds which equal or exceed the GNP of some smaller nations. Basic research is not achieved by throwing money at a problem; the critical variable is talented people. Painstaking cultivation over years is indispensable to perform basic research—something which few countries can do.

If a large U.S. corporation develops say 100 inventions a year, it uses only a very small fraction, such as 5 percent, to either improve its present products or to develop new ones. Why? Because the top ranking inventions (100, 99, 98, 97, 96) yield the most profitable innovations. If the corporation invests say $1.5 billion in R&D, the innovations based on the five inventions must yield $3 to $5 billion, or $1 billion per invention.

Inventions 100-96 each yields $1 billion or more. Invention 95, which the corporation chooses not to use may potentially yield not quite $1 billion, but say $0.9 billion. Similarly, inventions 94, 93, . . . 1.

Fig. 11.2
Applications in Superconductivity

High Magnetic Fields

H_{c2}: up to 200 kG

- High Energy Physics

- Fusion

- Nuclear Magnetic Resonance
  Tomography

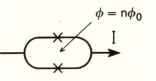

Coils

Quantum Interferometers

- Biomagnetism

- Detectors for Gravitational
  Waves

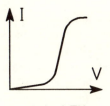

$\phi = n\phi_0$

I

$\phi_0 = 2 \times 10^{-7}$ Gauss·cm^2

Analog Electronics

- Microwave Detectors

- Signal Processors

- Voltage Normals

I

V

up to 1 THz

Digital Computer Elements

To protect the market of inventions 100–96, the corporation must deny the use of competing inventions 95-1 to competitors. As we said earlier, the corporation has a period of six months to two years in which to earn the $3-5 billion. During that period, other corporations at home and aboard shall have caught up and even surpassed the five inventions.

The heavy investment in R&D by the corporation continues in year 2. Let us say that the corporation produces 75 more inventions. The most profitable inventions are inventions with ranks 175–165. They are selected for use in year 2 and beyond, and inventions 164–1 are locked up with the exception of ranks 100–96 chosen in year 1.

Motivation 3: Imperative Need of NICs for U.S. Hi-Tech

While the large U.S. corporations are forced to lock up the vast majority of their inventions to protect the market of the select few inventions, the NICs, for all their enterprise, cannot ever hope to equal the sustained investment in R&D in so many fields. The logical sources of hi-tech are the United States, West Germany, and Japan.

Motivation 4: NIC Piracy of U.S. Intellectual Property Rights

Apparently with little recognition of the enormous risks of failure taken by large U.S. corporations when they invest billions in R&D each year, several NICs have pirated the fruits of their R&D. IBM took 11 Taiwan companies to court for violating their intellectual property rights; seven settled out of court and the other four were found guilty by courts in Taiwan.

We may view the acts of piracy as a desperate declaration of the dependency of the NICs on U.S. hi-tech. Can the obvious need of the NICs for U.S. hi-tech be met in a manner which is mutually satisfactory to the U.S. corporation and the NIC?

To apply the concomitant coalition process to the trade and technology between the United States and Taiwan, we need first to identify the areas of bargaining.

Areas of Bargaining (Why?)

Taiwan and the United States want to maximize their share of world trade. To enhance trade in the long term, Taiwan needs to import high (and high-er) technology from the United States in the short term.

Without high protection for high technology, Taiwan cannot expect the U.S. private sector to export hi-tech to Taiwan. Owing to the extreme importance attached to the protection of intellectual property rights, we can say that the United States is N-positive on intellectual property rights protection.

There are two sets of CONCOLs: the private sector in the United States; the private sector in Taiwan (Republic of China-ROC); the public sector in the United States; the public sector in ROC.

ROC public sector alter ego With long-term growth With abridgement of national rights

ROC public sector anti-ego Against long-term growth Against abridgement of national rights

ROC private sector alter ego With long-term growth Against intellectual property rights violation

ROC private sector anti-ego With short-term gains With intellectual property violations

What are the initial values of the index of imperativeness? It seems reasonable to say that the ROC public sector alter ego is N-positive on long-term growth;

so is the ROC private sector alter ego. The ROC public sector alter ego is also N-positive against intellectual property violations; so is the ROC private sector alter ego.

With both the public and private sector alter egos N-positive against intellectual property rights violations, why is it that the problem remains as serious as it is? It is because the anti-egos in both the public and private sectors are N-positive for intellectual property rights.

Measures of Outcome (What?)

The process of negotiation attempts to move opposing initial situations from the N-positive zone toward the N-zero zone. Thus, when the ROC public sector alter ego is N-positive in opposing intellectual property violations, and the ROC public sector anti-ego is N-positive in advocating intellectual property violations, how can a move toward the N-zero zone be achieved?

R&D Measures, Technology, Territory Measures

We have developed a set of specific measures of outcome in CONCOL situations, both within the same party and between parties:

R&D Measures 1–6

Technology Measures 1–5

Territory Measures 1–4

We will now develop a territory-technology measure which is especially germane to international technology transfer.

Territory-Technology Outcome: PS/PG Ratio

In current state-of-the-art of robotics, precision performance by say, a million cars off the robotics factory, is quite feasible. Every single one of the million cars will largely conform to general characteristics. The gear-ratio, the drag coefficient, the acceleration, the deceleration, and so forth of car no. 53 will be hardly distinguishable from car no. 1457 or from car no. 99,999, or any other car. All of them exhibit general performance characteristics, in the sense that the performance characteristics are common to all the million cars, and not unique to any one of them. We say that the million cars are performance general (PG) products.

Even with PG products, a certain amount of customization takes place. With future-generation computer technology, customization of car performance characteristics themselves is possible. The more the customization, the less the car will share characteristics with other cars; they are therefore, performance-specific (PS) products.

The more the hi-tech transfer, the higher the PS/PG ratio. While it is a country measure of outcome, the E/D ratio is a company measure of outcome.

Changes by Bargaining (How?)

Specific values can be associated with each of the ratios. For instance, the initial value of PS/PG may be 0.00. To avoid the mathematical problem of indeterminateness in the PS/PG ratio, we will use 0.01 instead of zero. Expressing the ratio as a percentage, we have the initial value of PS/PG as .01 × 100 = 1%. The desired outcome in a given time period can be chosen by the ROC, say 5.0. To move from 1 to 5 percent, what types of technology should be imported and from which companies?

An inducement to the XYZ company in the United States to transfer hi-tech to the ABC company in the ROC is the rise in the E/D value of ABC company from the initial 1 percent to the desired value, say of 7 percent. We have discussed at length how a part of XYZ company's income should be directly related to the sliding scale of share of sales revenue from exports by ABC of products imbedding the XYZ hi-tech.[5]

With the initial value and the desired outcome, the bargaining process can commence. The purpose of the bargaining is to move the CONCOL participants from the extreme position of N-positive to the middle zone of N-zero, which may be accomplished by several means.

Clarification of Extremes

If the XYZ company feels that it would jeopardize its precious technological assets if they are transferred without a specific commitment by the ROC government to honor the intellectual property rights, that position must be conveyed to the US public sector, ROC public sector, and ROC private sector.

Similarly, the XYZ company should convey unequivocally its position that the product(s) imbedding the hi-tech should not be sold in the U.S. market or the European market.

If the access to the United States and the European markets are N-positive issues for the ROC, it should convey that position clearly to the U.S. public sector and the U.S. private sector.

Modification of Extremes

There are degrees of N-positive positions. For instance, the credible protection of intellectual property rights is a nonnegotiable N-positive position. But, how about the access to the European market of the product(s) imbedding the hi-tech? Would the embargo be conditional or would the XYZ company modify it in time—say, after six months or after 18 months? Again, would the XYZ company agree to let ROC exporters access the European markets in six months if they do not export the product(s) to U.S. markets for five years?

Verification of Values

How credible is the ABC company's claim that E/D will rise to 7 percent? Since the market share is in the future, and relates to a future product, the XYZ company needs to be convinced that the figure is reasonable and reliable. To verify the reasonableness of the market share figure, the method of forecasting used by the ABC company needs to be presented, examined, and tested. The testing may have to be done on situations which could be considered similar. The central issues of the promises of the product market are the credibility of the premises and the processing of data.

Quid Pro Quo

The CONCOL participants could reduce the degree of N-positive positions of some elements (e.g., unused asset of inventions) in return for increasing the degree of N-positive issues of some other elements (e.g., access to the U.S. market). They could also trade some N-zero elements for N-positive or N-negative elements. It should be noted that the very process of bargaining could possibly change the relative index of imperativeness of the elements.

CONCLUDING OBSERVATIONS

We have discussed two applications of CONCOL: technology and territory. The former refers to IBM's policy of developing new technology; the latter to a CONCOL process of technology transfer from multinationals to NICs.

In CONCOL terms, IBM pursues two opposing interests with respect to technology: "improvement of current mainstream technology" and "the single most promising radical alternative" to it. In our terminology, IBM promotes linear extensions and quantum jumps simultaneously. Clearly, the funds devoted to one cannot be used for the other. The former is proven; continuing improvements of a product (process) are far more likely than success with its most promising radical alternative. In fact, the 1983 radical alternative of Josephson superconducting technology was subsequently set aside, indicating the very uncertainty of outcome of frontier research.

Superconductivity research achieved dramatic breakthroughs at IBM laboratories in 1987. The linear extension of $0.2667K$ a year for 75 years was displaced dramatically by a 56-fold increase in 1986, followed by a 337-fold increase in 1987. Undoubtedly, the accelerating pace of quantum jumps would significantly alter IBM R&D strategy.

IBM and other multinationals continue to accumulate inventions every year. Only a small fraction of these inventions can be profitably imbedded in products and processes, requiring the vast majority of inventions to be locked away from competition.

On an illustrative scale, NICs are at level 15, while the technology being used by the multinational is at level 100. Some NICs pirate the level-100 technology— which cannot be sustained for long because the multinationals would not permit their hard-earned inventions to be stolen from them. There is opposition of interests between the multinationals and the NICs. Can there be an area of bargaining which would be to mutual benefit?

While level-100 technology would not be licensed by the multinational, the NIC could well use say, level-45 technology, which would raise to 300 percent the NIC's technology level. The NIC does not have to risk a single R&D dollar; it does not have to train, hire, and employ researchers. It can directly license the technology.

In return for licensing, the multinational could insist that the NIC imbed the level-45 technology in a new product(s), and develop a market overseas. The multinational would receive licensing fees and a share of the new market revenues. A sliding scale of market share payments could encourage the NIC to increase its market.

If in 6 months the NIC has observed the letter and spirit of the technology transfer arrangement, the multinational would transfer a higher level technology, level 60, which raises the technology level of the NIC to 400 percent. The technology transfer would increase the market (territory).

CONCOL offers an analytic framework which recognizes the opposing interests on R&D investment within a corporation itself, between a corporation and a country, and between countries. It specifies a bargaining process that can achieve mutually beneficial results.

Notes

PREFACE

1. Ronald Reagan, "Strategic Defense Initiative," Address to the Nation, March 23, 1983, cited in *The President's Strategic Initiative*, U.S. Government Printing Office, 1985: 20940, January 1985, p. 1.

2. Herman Khan, *Thinking about the Unthinkable*, Avon, New York, 1985.

CHAPTER 1

1. Michael Schrage and Warren Brown, "GM: Chrome to Computers," part 2, *The Washington Post*, July 5, 1984, A4.

2. Ruben F. Mettler, "The Little Brown Hen That Could: The Growth Story of TRW Inc," Newcomen Society in North America, New York, 1982, 7.

3. Ibid., 23.

4. Ibid., 20, 22.

5. Edward Feigenbaum and Pamela McCordick, *The Fifth Generation: Artificial Intelligence and Japan's Computer Challenge to the World*, Addison-Wesley, Reading, Mass., 1983.

6. Reuters, "Semiconductor Trade Friction Looms on the Horizon as World Demand Slumps," *The Korea Times*, August 3, 1985, 9.

7. Winston S. Churchill, *The Grand Alliance*, Houghton Mifflin, Cambridge, Mass., 1951, 45.

8. Winston S. Churchill, *The Gathering Storm*, Houghton Mifflin, Cambridge, Mass., 1948, 149.

9. Winston S. Churchill, *Their Finest Hour*, Houghton Mifflin, Cambridge, Mass., 1949, 382.

10. Churchill, *Gathering Storm*, 158.

11. Churchill, *Their Finest Hour*, 382.

12. Ronald W. Clark, *Einstein: The Life and Times*, World, New York, 1971, 558.

13. Einstein–Roosevelt correspondence, Aug. 2, 1939, Roosevelt Library, Hyde Park.

14. Bohr-Chadwick, quoted in Cockroft, *Biographical Memoirs of Fellows of the Royal Society*, Vol. 9, London, 45.

15. William A. Ganoe, *A History of the United States Army*, Eric Lundberg, Ashton, Md., 1964, 516.

16. John F. Kennedy, Address to the Joint Session of Congress, May 21, 1961.

17. Hugh Sidey, *John F. Kennedy, Portrait of a President*, Deutsch, Germany, 1964.

18. Ronald Reagan, "Presidential Foreword," in *The President's Strategic Initiative*, U.S. Government Printing Office, Wash., D.C., 1985, i.

19. John A. Adam and Paul Wallich, "Mind-boggling Complexity," IEEE *Spectrum*, Vol. 22, No. 9, Sept. 1985, 85, 36.

20. Churchill, *Gathering Storm*, 148.

21. SDI Office, "The Strategic Defense Initiative," Pentagon, 1985.

22. Lt. Gen. James A. Abrahamson, "Statement on the Strategic Defense Initiative," U.S. Senate Armed Services Committee, Oct. 30, 1985, 11.

23. Patrick E. Haggerty, *Management Philosophies and Practices of Texas Instruments Incorporated*, Texas Instruments, Dallas, Tex. 1965, 50.

24. Ibid., 17.

25. Ibid., 53–54.

26. Patrick E. Haggerty, Interview in *Innovation*. No. 8, 1964, 31.

27. J.-J. Servan-Schreiber, *The American Challenge*, Atheneum, New York, 1968, 138.

CHAPTER 2

1. National Science Foundation, *National Patterns of R&D Resources 1953–75*, NSF 70–46, Wash., D.C., 1970, 24–25.

2. National Science Foundation, *Science, Technology, and Innovation*, Wash., D.C. 1973, 2.

3. Ibid., 3.

4. Ibid., 10–11.

5. Fred Hiatt and Rick Atkinson, "Arms and America's Fortunes," *The Washington Post*, Dec. 1, 1985, Al.

6. Ibid., A20.

7. Ibid.

8. Ibid.

9. Colin Norman, "Science Escapes Brunt of Budget Ax," *Science*, Vol. 231, Feb. 21, 1986, 786–87.

10. Frank Press, "Science: The Best and Worst of Times," *Science*, Vol 231, Mar. 21, 1986, 135.

11. National Science Foundation, *Science Indicators—The 1985 Report*, Wash., D.C., 1986.

12. Erich Bloch, "Basic Research and Economic Health: The Coming Challenge," *Science*, Vol. 232, May 2, 1986, 396.

13. Ibid., 198.

14. J.-J Servan-Schreiber and Herbert A. Simon, "America Must Continue to be the World's University," *The Washington Post*, Nov. 29, 1987, D1.

CHAPTER 3

1. Richard N. Foster, "Why America's Technology Leaders Tend to Lose," *Vital Speeches of the Day*, June 15, 1983, 524–26.
2. Patrick E. Haggerty, *Management Philosophies and Practices of Texas Instruments Incorporated*, Texas Instruments, Dallas, Tex., 1965, 50.
3. John von Neumann and Oskar Morgenstern, *Theory of Games and Economic Behavior*, Princeton University Press, Princeton, N.J., 1944.
4. George K. Chacko, "Bargaining Strategy in a Production and Distribution Problem," *Operations Research*, Nov.–Dec. 1961, 185–87.
5. *Survey of Current Business*, monthly.
6. Richard N. Foster, "Why America's Technology Leaders Tend to Lose," *Vital Speeches of the Day*, June 15, 1983, 526.
7. Edwin Mansfield et al., *Research and Innovation in the Modern Corporation*, Norton, New York, 1971, chap. 3.

CHAPTER 4

1. United Press International, "Japanese Trade Envoy in U.S.," *The China Post*, Taipei, Taiwan, April 5, 1985, 1.
2. Reuters, "U.S. Congress Warns of Trade Retaliation," *The China Post*, April 4, 1985, 1.
3. Associated Press, "U.S. Senators Press for Retaliatory Action Against Japanese Imports," *The China Post*, Mar. 22, 1985, 5.
4. Defense Advanced Research Projects Agency, "Strategic Computing," Wash., D.C., Oct. 1983.
5. General Accounting Office, "Support for Development of Electronics and Materials Technologies by the Governments of the United States, Japan, West Germany, France, and the United Kingdom," GAO/RECED 85–63, Wash., D.C., Sep. 9, 1985, 1.
6. Arthur L. Robinson, "A Chemical Route to Advanced Ceramics," *Science*, Vol. 233, July 4, 1986, 25.
7. Ibid.
8. Ibid., 25–26.

CHAPTER 6

1. Patrick E. Haggerty, *Management Philosophies and Practices of Texas Instruments Incorporated*, Texas Instruments, Dallas, Tex., 1965, 50.
2. Jack A. Morton, "From Research to Technology," in David Allison (ed.), *The R&D Game*, MIT, Cambridge, Mass., 1969, 219–21.
3. Haggerty, *Management Philosophies and Practices*, 53–54.
4. Ibid.
5. Ibid.

6. Daniel J. Boorstin, *The Americans: The Democratic Experience*, Random House, New York, 1973, 401.

7. John H. Dessauer, *My Years with Xerox*, Manor, New York, 1971, 4.

8. Ibid, 49.

9. Ibid., 43.

10. Boorstin, *Americans*, 401.

11. Dessauer, *My Years with Xerox*, 43.

12. Ibid.

13. Patrick E. Haggerty, Interview in *Innovation*, No. 8, 1969, 52–53.

14. Dessauer, *My Years with Xerox*, 42.

15. Albert Einstein, "Atomic War or Peace," *Atlantic Monthly*, Nov. 1945.

16. Bohr-Chadwick, quoted in Cockroft, *Biographical Memoirs of Fellows of Royal Society*, Vol. 9, London, 45.

17. Leslie R. Groves, *Now It Can Be Told*, Da Capo Press, New York, 1975, 5, 6.

18. Einstein-Roosevelt correspondence, Aug. 2, 1939, Roosevelt Library, Hyde Park.

19. Ronald W. Clark, *Einstein: The Life and Times*, World, New York, 1971, 558.

20. Groves, *Now It Can Be Told*, 4.

21. Ibid., 19–20.

22. Ibid., 11.

23. Conant-Bush letter, quoted in Stephanie Groueff, *Manhattan Project: The Untold Story of the Making of the Atomic Bomb*, Little, Brown, Boston, 1967, 12 n.

24. Groves, *Now It Can Be Told*, 360.

25. William A. Ganoe, *A History of the United States Army*, Eric Lundberg, Ashton, Md., 1964, 516.

CHAPTER 7

1. David Irving, *The German Atomic Bomb*, Simon & Schuster, New York, 1967, 305–20.

2. Ibid., 83, 151.

3. Albert Speer, *Inside the Third Reich*, quoted in David Irving.

4. Irving, *German Atomic Bomb*, 36–37.

5. Ibid., 42, 35, 43, 45, 25.

6. Speer, *Inside the Third Reich*.

7. Irving, *German Atomic Bomb*, 241.

8. Ibid., 104–5.

9. Daniel Lang, *From Hiroshima to the Moon*, Simon & Schuster, New York, 1959, 183–84.

10. Speer, *Inside the Third Reich*.

11. Irving, *German Atomic Bomb*, 172, 232.

12. Ibid., 102.

13. Ibid., 296.

14. Ibid., 295–96.

15. Ibid., 102.

16. Morton Grodzins and Sugine Rabinowitch (eds.), *The Atomic Age*, Basic Books, New York, 1963, 28–29.

17. Richard N. Foster, "Why America's Technology Leaders Tend to Lose," *Vital Speeches of the Day*, June 15, 1983, 526.

18. Jack A. Morton, "From Research to Technology," in David Allison (ed.), *The R&D Game*, Cambridge, Mass., 1969, 219–21.

19. Foster, "Why America's Technology Leaders Tend to Lose," 526.

20. Ibid.

21. Ibid., 525.

22. Ibid.

23. Ibid, 526.

CHAPTER 8

1. TRW, *Nineteen Hundred and Sixty Eight Annual Report to Investors*, TRW, Inc., Cleveland, Ohio, 1968, inside cover.

2. Patrick E. Haggerty, "Objectives, Strategies, and Tactics," Presentation to Texas Instruments Annual Planning Conference, December 1962, 13.

3. Raymond S. Isenson, "Technological Forecasting Lessons from Project Hindsight," in James R. Bright (ed.), *Technological Forecasting for Industry and Government*, Prentice-Hall, Englewood Cliffs, N.J. 1968, 39–40.

4. National Science Foundation, *Science, Technology and Innovation*, Wash., D.C., 1973, 8.

5. P. Ranganath Nyak and John M. Ketteringham, *Breakthroughs!*, Rawson, New York 1986, 344, 17.

6. NSF, *Science, Technology and Innovation*, 8.

7. Nyak and Ketteringham, *Breakthroughs!*, 358.

8. Maurice E. Esch, "Honeywell's PATTERN: Planning Assistance Through Technical Evaluation of Relevance Numbers," Paper presented at the 17th National Aerospace Electronics Conference, Dayton, Ohio, May 10-12, 1965.

9. Richard Foster, *Innovation—The Attacker's Advantage*, Simon & Schuster, New York, 1986, 123–24.

10. Ibid, 124–25.

11. Richard Foster, "Why America's Technology Leaders Tend to Lose," *Vital Speeches of the Day*, June 15, 1983, 525.

CHAPTER 10

1. Strobe Talbot (tr. and ed.), *Khrushchev Remembers*, Little, Brown, Boston, 1947, 49–98.

2. Ibid., 495–96.

3. Kenichi Ohmae, "A Japanese View," *The Washington Post*, Nov. 1, 1987, C2.

4. Ibid.

CHAPTER 11

1. Richard Foster, "Why America's Technology Leaders Tend to Lose," *Vital Speeches of the Day*, June 15, 1983, 525.

2. Lewis Branscomb, "Research and Development: Key Issues for Management," The Conference Board, No. 842, 1983.

3. K. Alex Muller and J. Georg Bednorz, ''The Discovery of a Class of High-Temperature Superconductors,'' *Science*, Vol. 237, Sept. 4, 1987, 1133–4.

4. Ibid.

5. George K. Chacko, *Trade Drain Imperative of Technology Transfer: U.S.-Taiwan Concomitant Coalitions*, National Chengchi University, Taipei and Petrocelli, Princeton, N.J., 1985, Chap. 10.

Bibliography

Abrahamson, Lt. Gen. "Statement on the Strategic Initiative," U.S. Senate Armed Services Committee, Oct. 30, 1985.

Adam, John A., and Paul Wallich. "Mind-boggling Complexity," IEEE *Spectum*, Vol. 22, No. 9, Sep. 1985.

Allison, David (ed.). *The R&D Game*, MIT, Cambridge, 1969.

Associated Press. "U.S. Senators Press for Retaliatory Action Against Japanese Imports," *The China Post*, Taiwan, Mar. 22, 1985.

Atkinson, Rick. See Hiatt, Fred, and Rick Atkinson.

Bloch, Erich. "Basic Research and Economic Health: The Coming Challenge," *Science*, Vol. 232, May 2, 1986.

Bohr-Chadwick. See Cockroft.

Boorstin, Daniel J. *The Americans: The Democratic Experience*, Random House, New York, 1973.

Branscomb, Lewis. "Research and Development: Key Issues for Management," The Conference Board, No. 842, 1983.

Bright, James R. (ed.). *Technological Forecasting for Industry and Government*, Prentice-Hall, Englewood Cliffs, N.J., 1968.

Brown, Warren. See Schrage, Michael, and Warren Brown.

Chacko, George K. "Bargaining Strategy in a Production and Distribution Problem," *Operations Research*, Nov.–Dec. 1961.

———. *Trade Drain Imperative of Technology Transfer: U.S.-Taiwan Concomitant Coalitions*, National Chengchi University, Taipei and Petrocelli, Princeton, N.J., 1985.

Churchill, Winston S. *The Gathering Storm*, Houghton Mifflin, Cambridge, Mass., 1948.

———. *Their Finest Hour*, Houghton Mifflin, Cambridge, Mass., 1949.

———. *The Grand Alliance*, Houghton Mifflin, Cambridge, Mass., 1951.

Clark, Ronald W. *Einstein: The Life and Times*, World, New York, 1971.

Cockroft. *Biographical Memoirs of Fellows of the Royal Society*, Royal Society, Vol. 9, London.

Conant-Bush letter. See Groueff, Stephanie.

Defense Advanced Research Projects Agency. "Strategic Computing," Wash., D.C., Oct. 1983.

Dessauer, John H. *My Years with Xerox*, Manor, New York, 1971.

Einstein, Albert. "Atomic War or Peace," *Atlantic Monthly*, Nov. 1945.

Einstein–Roosevelt correspondence. Aug. 2, 1939, Roosevelt Library, Hyde Park.

Esch, Maurice E. "Honeywell's PATTERN: Planning Through Technical Evaluation of Relevance Numbers," Paper presented at the 17th National Aerospace Electronics Conference, Dayton, Ohio, May 10–12, 1965.

Feigenbaum, Edward, and Pamela McCordick. *The Fifth Generation: Artificial Intelligence and Japan's Computer Challenge to the World*, Addison-Wesley, Reading, Ma., 1983.

Foster, Richard N. "Why America's Technology Leaders Tend to Lose," *Vital Speeches of the Day*, June 25, 1984.

———. *Innovation—The Attacker's Advantage*, Simon & Schuster, New York, 1986.

Ganoe, William A. *A History of the United States Army*, Eric Lundberg, Ashton, Md., 1964.

General Accounting Office. "Support for Development of Electronics and Materials Technologies by the Governments of the United States, Japan, West Germany, France, and the United Kingdom," GAO/RECED 85–63, Wash., D.C., Sept. 9, 1985.

Grodzins, Morton, and Sugine Rabinowitch (eds.). *The Atomic Age*, Basic Books, New York, 1963.

Groueff, Stephanie. *Manhattan Project: The Untold Story of the Making of the Atomic Bomb*, Little, Brown, Boston, 1967.

Groves, Leslie R. *Now It Can Be Told*, Da Capo Press, New York, 1975.

Haggerty, Patrick E. *Management Philosophies and Practices of Texas Instruments Incorporated*, Texas Instruments, Dallas, Tex. 1965.

Hiatt, Fred, and Rick Atkinson. "Arms and America's Fortunes," *The Washington Post*, Dec. 1, 1985.

Irving, David. *The German Atomic Bomb*, Simon & Schuster, New York, 1967.

Isenson, Raymond S. "Technological Forecasting Lessons from Project Hindsight." In James R. Bright, (ed.), *Technological Forecasting for Industry and Government*, Prentice-Hall, Englewood Cliffs, N.J., 1968, 39–40.

Jantsch, Erich, *Technological Forecasting in Perspective* OECD, Paris, 1967.

Kennedy, John F. Address to the Joint Session of Congress, May 21, 1961.

Ketteringham, John M. See Nyak, P. Ranganath, and John M. Ketteringham.

Khan, Herman. *Thinking About the Unthinkable*, Avon, New York, 1958.

Lang, Daniel. *From Hiroshima to the Moon*, Simon & Schuster, New York, 1959.

McCordick, Pamela. See Feignbaum, Edward, and Pamela McCordick.

Mansfield, Edwin, et al. *Research and Innovation in the Modern Corporation*, Norton, New York, 1971.

Martino, Joseph. *Technological Forecasting for Decision-making*, North-Holland, Amsterdam, The Netherlands, 1983.

Mettler, Ruben F. "The Little Brown Hen That Could: The Growth Story of TRW Inc.," Newcomen Society in North America, New York, 1982.

Morgenstern, Oskar. See John von Neumann and Oskar Morgenstern.

Morton, Jack A. "From Research to Technology." In David Allison (ed.), *The R&D Game*, MIT, Cambridge, Ma., 1969.

Muller, K. Alex, and Georg Bednorz. "The Discovery of a Class of High-Temperature Superconductors, "*Science*, Vol. 237, Sep. 4, 1987.

National Science Foundation. *National Patterns of R&D Resources 1953–75*, NSF 70–46, Wash., D.C., 1970

———. *Science, Technology and Innovation*, Wash., D.C., 1973.

———. *National Patterns of Science and Technology Resources 1986*, NSF 86–309, Wash., D.C., 1986.

———. *Foreign Citizens in U.S. Science and Engineering: History, Status, and Outlook*, NSF 86–305 revised, Wash., D.C., 1986.

———. *Science Indicators—The 1985 Report*, Wash., D.C., 1986.

Norman, Colin. "Science Escapes Brunt of Budget Ax," *Science*, Vol. 231, Feb. 21, 1986.

Nyak, P. Ranganath, and John M. Ketteringham. *Breakthroughs!* Rawson, New York, 1986.

Ohmae, Kenichi. "A Japanese View," *The Washington Post*, Nov. 1, 1987.

Press, Frank. "Science: The Best and Worst of Times," *Science*, Vol. 231, Mar. 21, 1986.

Reagan, Ronald. "Presidential Foreword," In *The President's Strategic Initiative*, U.S. Government Printing Office, Wash., D.C., 1985.

Reuters. "Semiconductor Trade Friction Looms on the Horizon as World Demand Slumps," *The Korea Times*, Aug. 3, 1985.

———. "U.S. Congress Warns of Trade Retaliation," *The China Post*, April 4, 1985.

Robinson, Arthur L. "A Chemical Route to Advanced Ceramics," *Science*, Vol. 233, July 4, 1986.

Schrage, Michael, and Warren Brown. "GM: Chrome to Computers," part 2, *The Washington Post*, July 5, 1984.

Servan-Schreiber, J.-J. *The American Challenge*, Atheneum, New York, 1968.

Servan-Schreiber, J.-J, and Herbert A. Simon. "America Must Continue as World's University," *The Washington Post*, Nov. 29, 1987.

Sidey, Hugh. *John F. Kennedy, Portrait of a President*, Deutsch, Germany, 1964.

Simon, Herbert A. See Servan-Schreiber, J.-J, and Herbert A. Simon.

SDI Office, "Report to Congress on the Strategie Defense Initiative," Pentagon, 1985.

Survey of Current Business, monthly.

Talbot, Strobe (tr. and ed.). *Khrushchev Remembers*, Little, Brown, Boston, 1947.

TRW. *Nineteen Hundred and Sixty Eight Annual Report to Investors*, TRW, Inc., Cleveland, Ohio, 1968.

United Press International. "Japanese Trade Envoy in U.S.," *The China Post*, Taipei, Taiwan, April 5, 1985.

von Neumann, John, and Oskar Morgenstern. *Theory of Games and Economic Behavior*, Princeton University Press, Princeton, N.J., 1944.

Zwicky, Fnitz. *Morphology of Propulsive Power*, California Institute of Technology Bookstore, Pasadina, Ca., 1962.

Index

ABOUT THE AUTHOR

GEORGE K. CHACKO is Professor of Systems Science at the University of Southern California in Los Angeles and Director of the Doctoral Program in Technology Management at National Chengchi University in Taipei. Previously, he has held positions in research and management with Union Carbide, Hughes Aircraft, and TRW Systems, and has twice been named to the Senior Fulbright Professorship in Taiwan.

A Member of the World Future Society and Fellow of the American Association for the Advancement of Science and the American Astronautical Society, Dr. Chacko is the author of some 35 books, including *Dynamic Program Management* (Praeger, 1989). He earned a B.Comm. from Calcutta University, an M.A. from Madras University, and a Ph.D. from the New School for Social Research.